The Great Fire

JIM MURPHY

The Great Fire

SCHOLASTIC
HARDCOVER

SCHOLASTIC INC.

New York

Library of Congress Cataloging-in-Publication Data

Murphy, Jim, 1947-
The great fire / Jim Murphy.
p.   cm.
Includes bibliographical references and index.
ISBN 0-590-47267-4
1. Fires — Illinois — Chicago — History — 19th century — Juvenile literature.
2. Chicago (Ill.) — History — To 1875 — Juvenile literature.
[1. Fires — Illinois — Chicago — History — 19th century.
2. Chicago (Ill.) — History — To 1875.] I. Title.
F548.42.M87   1995
977.3'11041 — dc20   94-9963
CIP
AC

12 11 10 9 8 7 6 5 4   6 7 8 9/9 0/0

Printed in the U.S.A.

First printing, April 1995

The display type was set in Penman Medium by WLCR New York, Inc.

The text type was set in Sabon by Monotype Composition Company, Inc., Baltimore MD

Printed and bound by Berryville Graphics, VA

Maps by Heather Saunders

Production supervision by Angela Biola

Design by Marijka Kostiw

Acknowledgements

I am indebted to a number of institutions and individuals for their kind help in putting this book together: the Art Institute of Chicago; the University of Chicago Libraries; the Chicago Architecture Foundation; the Chicago Historical Society; and the Chicago Public Library.

In addition, I wish to thank Lesley Martin for meticulously fact-checking the manuscript, Arthur Cohen for his skillful camerawork, and Charlie Hess for the many invaluable tours of his city.

*For Janet and Arthur —
good neighbors and good friends —
and for their son Lucas,
whose smile can light up a room.*

Contents

Introduction

T HE FIRE *that swept through the heart of Chicago began on Sunday night, October 8, 1871. The Great Fire would burn for the rest of Sunday, all of Monday, and into the early hours of Tuesday with little real opposition.*

During these thirty-one hours of terror, over 100,000 people were forced to flee the consuming flames. Many survivors wrote about their harrowing experiences in books, newspaper and magazine articles, or letters to friends and relatives. You will meet a number of survivors in this book, most of them just once or twice and only briefly. Several individuals have slightly longer accounts, including Catherine and Patrick O'Leary, in whose barn the fire began; James Hildreth, an ex-alderman who decided that the best way to save Chicago was by blowing up parts of it; and Julia Lemos, a widow who single-handedly saved her five small children and her elderly parents. Finally, you will be able to follow four characters in great detail. In order of appearance they are Joseph E. Chamberlin, a twenty-year-old reporter for the Chicago Evening Post; *Horace White, the editor in chief of the* Chicago Tribune; *Alexander Frear, who was visiting relatives at the time of the fire; and Claire Innes, a twelve year old whose family had only recently moved to the city. Through the eyes of all these people you will see the fire from many distinct vantage points, and feel a wide range of emotions as the hot breath of the fire draws nearer and nearer.*

1 · A City Ready to Burn

IT WAS SUNDAY and an unusually warm evening for October eighth, so Daniel "Peg Leg" Sullivan left his stifling little house in the West Side of Chicago and went to visit neighbors. One of his stops was at the shingled cottage of Patrick and Catherine O'Leary. The one-legged Sullivan remembered getting to the O'Learys' house at around eight o'clock, but left after only a few minutes because the O'Leary family was already in bed. Both Patrick and Catherine had to be up very early in the morning: he to set off for his job as a laborer; she to milk their five cows and then deliver the milk to neighbors.

Sullivan ambled down the stretch of land between the O'Learys' and their neighbor, crossed the street, and sat down on the wooden sidewalk in front of Thomas White's house. After adjusting his wooden leg to make himself comfortable, he leaned back against White's fence to enjoy the night.

The wind coming off the prairie had been strong all day, sometimes gusting wildly, and leaves scuttled along the street; the sound of laughter and fiddle music drifted through the night. A

137 De Koven Street — where it all began. The original cottage in front with the door open was the portion Catherine and Patrick O'Leary rented to Patrick McLaughlin. The O'Leary family lived in the addition in back with the window boarded up. Note the wooden sidewalk. (Chicago Historical Society)

party was going on at the McLaughlins' to celebrate the arrival of a relative from Ireland. Another neighbor, Dennis Rogan, dropped by the O'Learys' at eight-thirty, but he, too, left when he learned the family was in bed.

Fifteen minutes later, Sullivan decided to go home. As the driver of a wagon, he would need every ounce of strength come morning. It was while pushing himself up that Sullivan first saw the fire — a single tongue of flame shooting out the side of the O'Learys' barn.

Sullivan didn't hesitate a second. "FIRE! FIRE! FIRE!" he shouted as loudly as he could. Running clumsily across the dirt street, Sullivan made his way directly to the barn. There was no time to stop for help. The building was already burning fiercely and he knew that in addition to five cows, the O'Learys had a calf and a horse in there.

The barn's loft held over three tons of timothy hay, delivered earlier that day. Flames from the burning hay pushed against the roof and beams, almost as if they were struggling to break free. A shower of burning embers greeted Sullivan as he entered the building.

He untied the ropes of two cows, but the frightened animals did not move. On the other side of the barn, another cow and the horse were tied to the wall, straining to get loose. Sullivan took a step toward them, then realized that the fire had gotten around behind him and might cut off any chance of escape in a matter of seconds. The heat was fiercely intense and blinding, and in his rush to flee, Sullivan slipped on the uneven floorboards and fell with a thud.

He struggled to get up and, as he did, Sullivan discovered that his wooden leg had gotten stuck between two boards and come off. Instead of panicking, he began hopping toward where he thought the door was. Luck was with him. He had gone a few feet when the O'Learys' calf bumped into him, and Sullivan was able to throw his arms around its neck. Together, man and calf managed to find the door and safety, both frightened, both badly singed.

A shed attached to the barn was already engulfed by flames. It contained two tons of coal for the winter and a large supply of kindling wood. Fire ran along the dry grass and leaves, and took hold of a neighbor's fence. The heat from the burning barn, shed, and fence was so hot that the O'Learys' house, forty feet away, began to smolder. Neighbors rushed from their homes, many carrying buckets or pots of water. The sound of music and merrymaking stopped abruptly, replaced by the shout of "FIRE!" It would be a warning cry heard thousands of times during the next thirty-one hours.

An overhead view of Chicago as it appeared before the Great Fire. Lake Michigan is in the foreground, and the Chicago River branches left and right. The South Side is on the left, while the North Side is to the right. (Harper's Weekly, October 21, 1871)

16

The Chamber of Commerce Building before the fire. It was one of many buildings the citizens of Chicago pointed to with pride. Many of the fancy details (such as those above the clock) were really carved out of wood. In addition, the mansard roof was made of tar and wood. (Author's collection)

Chicago in 1871 was a city ready to burn. The city boasted having 59,500 buildings, many of them — such as the Courthouse and the *Tribune* Building — large and ornately decorated. The trouble was that about two-thirds of all these structures were made entirely of wood. Many of the remaining buildings (even the ones proclaimed to be "fireproof") looked solid, but were actually jerry-built affairs; the stone or brick exteriors hid wooden frames and floors, all topped with highly flammable tar or shingle roofs. It was also a common practice to disguise wood as another kind of building material. The fancy exterior decorations on just about every building were carved from wood, then painted to look like stone or marble. Most churches had steeples that appeared to be solid from the street, but a closer inspection would reveal a wooden framework covered with cleverly painted copper or tin.

The situation was worst in the middle-class and poorer districts. Lot sizes were small, and owners usually filled them up with cottages, barns, sheds, and outhouses — all made of fast-burning wood, naturally. Because both Patrick and Catherine O'Leary worked, they were able to put a large addition on their cottage despite a lot size of just 25 by 100 feet. Interspersed in these residential areas were a variety of businesses — paint factories, lumberyards, distilleries, gasworks, mills, furniture manufacturers, warehouses, and coal distributors.

Wealthier districts were by no means free of fire hazards. Stately stone and brick homes had wood interiors, and stood side by side with smaller wood-frame houses. Wooden stables and other storage buildings were common, and trees lined the streets and filled the yards.

The links between richer and poorer sections went beyond the materials used for construction or the way buildings were crammed together. Chicago had been built largely on soggy marshland that flooded every time it rained. As the years passed and the town developed, a quick solution to the water and mud problem was needed. The answer was to make the roads and sidewalks out of wood and elevate them above the waterline, in some places by several feet. On the day the fire started, over 55 miles of pine-block streets and 600 miles of wooden sidewalks bound the 23,000 acres of the city in a highly combustible knot.

Fires were common in all cities back then, and Chicago was no exception. In 1863 there had been 186 reported fires in Chicago; the number had risen to 515 by 1868. Records for 1870 indicate that fire-fighting companies responded to nearly 600 alarms. The next year saw even more fires spring up, mainly because the summer had been unusually dry. Between July and October only a few scattered showers had taken place and these did not produce much water at all. Trees drooped in the unrelenting summer sun; grass and leaves dried out. By October, as many as six fires were breaking out every day. On Saturday the seventh, the night before the Great Fire, a blaze destroyed four blocks and took over sixteen hours to control. What made Sunday the eighth different and particularly dangerous was the steady wind blowing in from the southwest.

It was this gusting, swirling wind that drove the flames from the O'Learys' barn into neighboring yards. To the east, a fence and shed of James Dalton's went up in flames; to the west, a barn smoldered for a few minutes, then flared up into a thousand yellow-orange fingers. Dennis Rogan had heard Sullivan's initial shouts about a fire and returned. He forced open the door to the O'Learys' house and called for them to wake up.

Moments later, Patrick emerged from the cottage, still half

This picture of Chicago in 1820 shows the open prairie stretching to the horizon.
(Author's collection)

Chicago was built on marshland as this scene from 1833 makes clear. As the city grew in size, the roads, sidewalks, and buildings were gradually raised to alleviate the muddy conditions. (Author's collection)

asleep. "Kate!" he screamed the moment he saw what was happening. "The barn is afire!"

Their first action was to get their children out of the house and into the street safely away from the fire. The barn was already engulfed in flames, so Patrick and a group of neighbors began pouring water on the cottage. It would catch fire several times during the night, but the flames would be smothered before they could get out of control. Strangely enough, the cottage on the O'Leary property would survive with little damage.

At about this time William Lee, who lived down the block from the O'Learys', went into his seventeen-month-old son's room to see why the child was crying. After comforting his son, Lee went to fasten the window blind. Outside, he saw a crimson night sky

lit up by flames and flying embers. Already some of those embers were landing in his yard and igniting the grass and leaves.

Lee hesitated a moment before shouting to his wife to take care of the baby and rushing out of the house. He ran the three blocks to Bruno Goll's drugstore, determined to do what no one else in the neighborhood had thought about doing: turn in a fire alarm. At this point, the fire was barely fifteen minutes old. What followed was a series of fatal errors that set the fire free and doomed the city to a fiery death.

Goll's drugstore to which William Lee raced to turn in a fire alarm. The picture is badly scratched, but someone has drawn a big arrow to point out the fire alarm box. No one in the picture has been identified, but it is possible that the man to the right is Bruno Goll. (Chicago Historical Society)

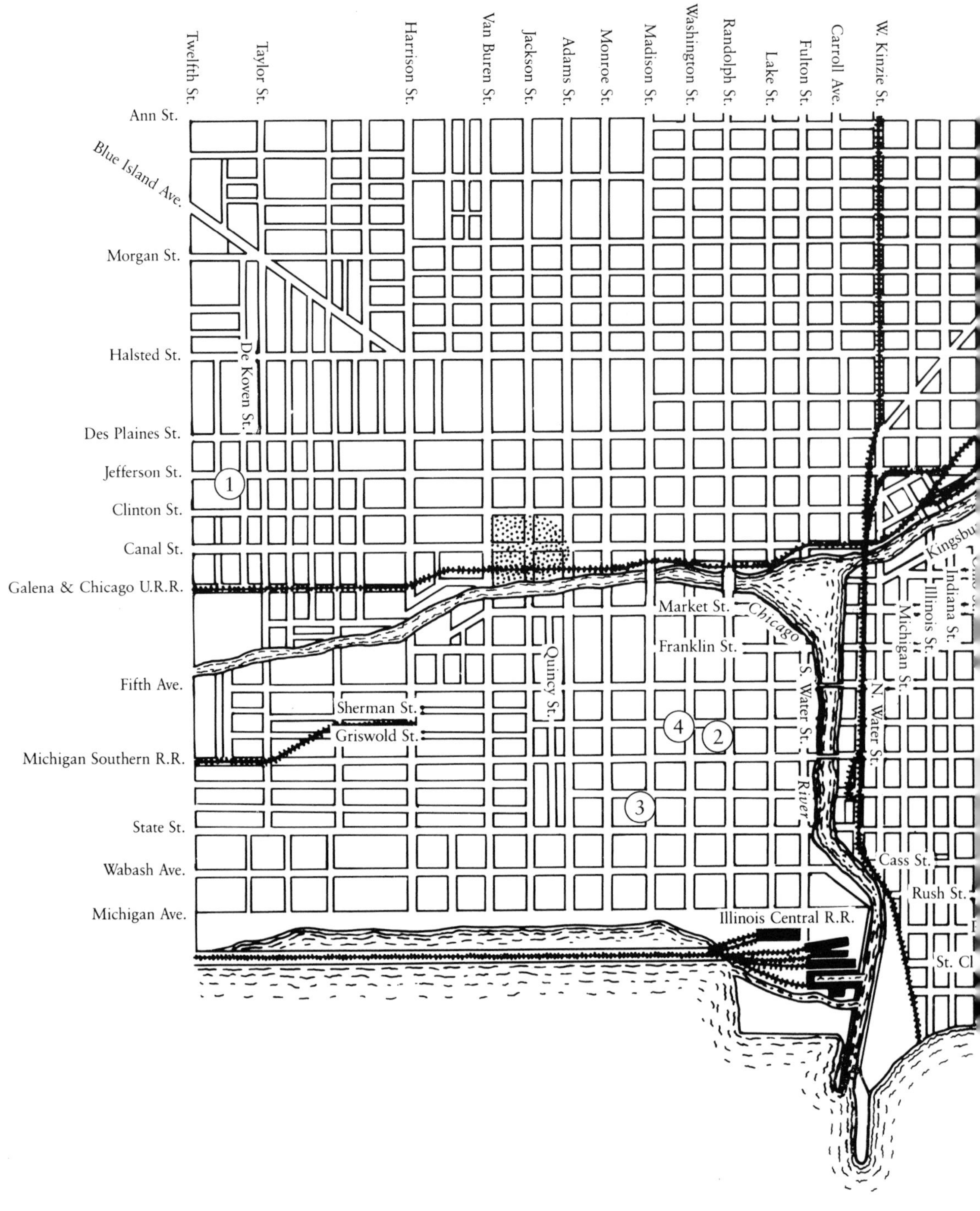
Twelfth St.
Taylor St.
Harrison St.
Van Buren St.
Jackson St.
Adams St.
Monroe St.
Madison St.
Washington St.
Randolph St.
Lake St.
Fulton St.
Carroll Ave.
W. Kinzie St.
Ann St.
Blue Island Ave.
Morgan St.
Halsted St.
De Koven St.
Des Plaines St.
Jefferson St.
Clinton St.
Canal St.
Galena & Chicago U.R.R.
Market St.
Chicago
Franklin St.
Quincy St.
Fifth Ave.
Sherman St.
Griswold St.
Michigan Southern R.R.
S. Water St.
River
N. Water St.
Kingsbu
Indiana St.
Illinois St.
Michigan St.
State St.
Wabash Ave.
Michigan Ave.
Cass St.
Rush St.
Illinois Central R.R.
St. Cl
1
2
3
4

Area destroyed by Saturday night's fire

1. Home of Patrick and Catherine O'Leary
2. Courthouse
3. *Tribune* Building
4. Chamber of Commerce Building

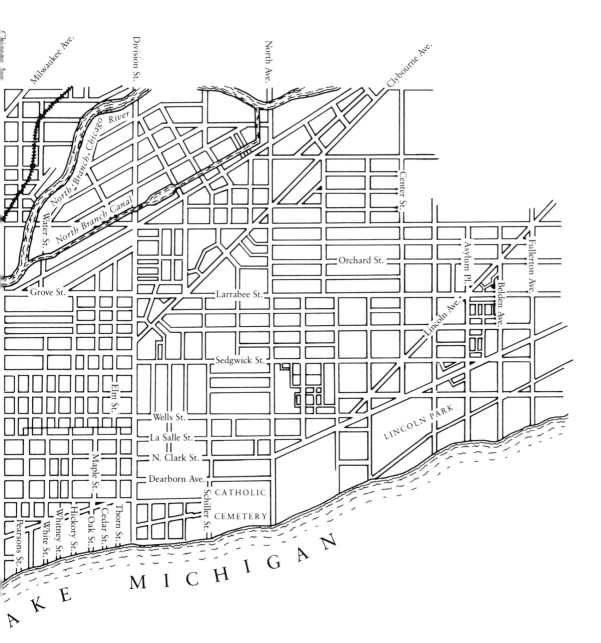

Milwaukee Ave.

Division St.

North Ave.

Clybourne Ave.

North Branch, Chicago River

North Branch Canal

Water St.

Center St.

Asylum Pl.

Fullerton Ave.

Orchard St.

Belden Ave.

Grove St.

Larrabee St.

Lincoln Ave.

Elm St.

Sedgwick St.

Wells St.

La Salle St.

LINCOLN PARK

N. Clark St.

Maple St.

Dearborn Ave.

Hickory St.

Cedar St.

Oak St.

Thorn St.

Schiller St.

CATHOLIC
CEMETERY

Whitney St.

White St.

Pearsons St.

LAKE MICHIGAN

Street map of sections destroyed by the fire. While the map shows only a small portion of the actual city of Chicago, this area was the chief business and cultural center, and housed nearly one third of its citizens.

2 · "Everything Went Wrong!"

WHEN WILLIAM LEE reached Goll's drugstore, he was gasping for air and frantic. In a breathless voice, Lee demanded the key to the alarm box that was mounted on the outside of the store. Bruno Goll refused to hand it over, insisting that a fire truck had already passed.

Lee had no time to argue with Goll. He was too concerned about the safety of his family, so he hurried back to them almost immediately. He got there just in time to see the fire taking hold of his neighbor's shed and fence, while the breeze blew a rain fire on his property. Two things were very clear to Lee: first, despite what Goll had said, no fire engines had arrived, and, second, his house was about to catch fire.

Lee's wife grabbed the baby and carried him outside, while Lee rounded up a few valuables and some food and put them in a cloth sack. The family fled to a vacant lot a block away where they spent the night watching the fire's terrible march. Oddly enough, the singed calf that "Peg Leg" Sullivan had helped escape came and stood by the Lees until dawn.

A steam pumper and crew race to a fire. (Author's collection)

As for Goll, he claimed later at the official inquiry into the fire that he had waited for Lee to leave and then turned in the alarm. Goll also insisted he turned in a second alarm when another man appeared ten minutes later to announce that the fire was spreading rapidly. Whether Goll lied about sending the alarms or whether the alarm box failed to work will never be known. What is clear, is that no alarm was recorded at the central alarm office in the Courthouse at the point when the fire was still containable.

A few minutes after the second man hurried away, Goll took off his apron, carefully extinguished the store's gaslights, and left, locking the door behind him. Like thousands of other people, he was on his way to De Koven Street to watch the fire.

While this was happening near the fire, more errors were taking

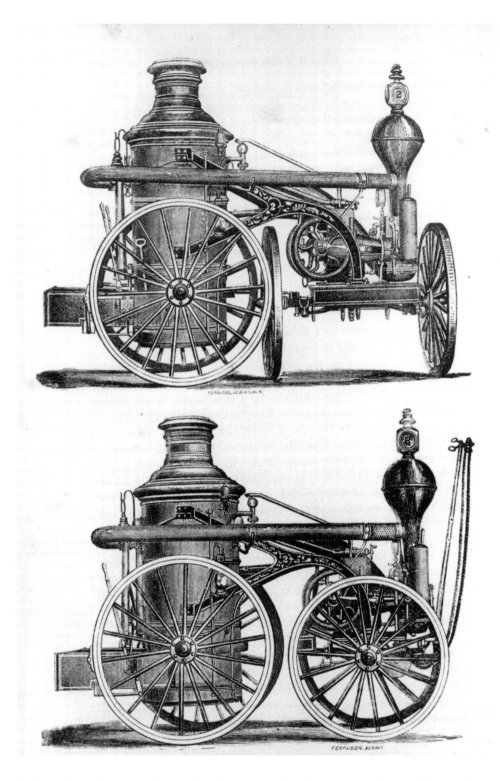

A side view of a steam fire engine that was designed and manufactured by L. Button & Son in Waterford, New York. Steam is created in the upright tubular boilers on the left, then channeled through copper pipes to the pumping engine at the front of the machine. This contraption weighed four thousand pounds but could throw water two hundred and thirty feet. (Author's collection)

place a mile and a half away. Chicago had recently renovated its fire alarm system, making it one of the best in the nation. Each firehouse had a watchman who scanned the immediate neighborhood for flames or smoke during the night. Overlooking the entire city was a watchman in the cupola of the Courthouse, one hundred feet above the ground. If a fire was spotted, an alarm was telegraphed (either from the firehouse or from one of the many alarm boxes situated around town) to the Courthouse; the Courthouse watchman then relayed the location of the blaze to the firehouses nearest to it. For added security, the giant Courthouse bell was also rung. Because of the drought, special Insurance Patrols had been organized and Benjamin Bullwinkle was appointed to head them. These patrols roamed the streets at night, ready to put out small fires with chemical extinguishers and turn in alarms for bigger blazes. While this system sounds very cumbersome to us, back in 1871 it was considered quite speedy and efficient.

On duty at the Courthouse that night was forty-year-old Mathias Schaffer. Schaffer was showing some visitors around the tower when one of them pointed to smoke in the distance. Schaffer glanced at the smoke, but dismissed the sighting. It was just the smoldering embers from the previous night's fire, he assured them. Nothing to worry about.

Several minutes passed before Schaffer looked up from what he was doing and saw flames leaping wildly into the black sky. The light *was* from a different fire after all; he'd been fooled because this new blaze was almost directly behind the still-flickering remnants of the Saturday October 7 fire.

He studied the flames, trying to determine their exact location. This wasn't easy because of the distance and tall buildings between him and the flames. In addition, the moonless sky was made even murkier by the swirling, smoky haze. Schaffer signaled down the speaking tube and had his assistant strike Box 342. This sent engines rumbling through the streets — to a location almost a mile away from the O'Learys' barn.

Schaffer's first signal went out at 9:30. Several minutes later,

With a statue of George Washington seemingly pointing the way, a steam engine clatters along a dark street. Since the boiler's coal fire was burning to make steam, residents had to be on the lookout for potentially dangerous sparks and cinders that often fell in the street. (Author's collection)

Schaffer realized his mistake and ordered Box 319 struck. This was still seven blocks away from the O'Learys', but close enough that firefighters could see the flames and alter their course. Unfortunately, Schaffer's young assistant, William J. Brown, stubbornly refused to strike Box 319, saying he was afraid it would confuse the situation. Brown was so stubborn about his decision that even after the fire he was able to write arrogantly in a letter that "I am still standing the watch that burned Chicago."

These errors had two fatal consequences. The most obvious was that a number of engines and dozens of firefighters were sent on a wild-goose chase and did not get to the fire for many minutes.

More critical is that it kept fire companies located near De Koven Street in their stations. Several had seen the eerie, dancing glow beyond the rooftops near them and, even without official notice from Schaffer, prepared to respond. When they heard Box 342 rung, however, they assumed the fire was out of their territory and unhitched the horses. Only two fire companies were not fooled by the misleading alarm.

As soon as the first shouts of "Fire!" were heard, scores of people swarmed toward De Koven Street. Many helped their neighbors fight the fire or drag furniture and clothes to the safety of the street. Most stood by watching the yellow-orange flames leaping from roof to roof and listening to the horrible *crackle pop* of dry pine being consumed. Fires were extremely common back then and thought to be as exciting and dramatic as a night at the theater.

One of the first to reach the fire was a twenty-year-old reporter for the *Chicago Evening Post* named Joseph E. Chamberlin. He'd been gathering information for a story, but the moment he spotted the new fire, he ran to see what was happening.

"I was at the scene in a few minutes," he recalled. "The fire had already advanced a distance of about a single square through the frame buildings that covered the ground thickly north of De Koven Street and east of Jefferson Street — if those miserable alleys shall be dignified by being denominated streets. That neighborhood had always been a *terra incognita* to respectable Chicagoans, and during a residence of three years in the city I had never visited it."

Chamberlin's distaste for the area and its inhabitants was shared by a great many people living in the city's wealthier sections and would go a long way toward fixing the blame for the Great Fire. The poor and slovenly people of De Koven Street — specifically Mrs. O'Leary and her cow — were the cause of the fire and the destruction of Chicago.

The clang of bells and the sound of pounding hooves could be heard above the roar of the fire. *America* arrived on the scene first, closely followed by *Little Giant*. Hoses were rolled out, attached

Even a small fire was a noisy experience, so fire marshals and steam engine foremen carried brass speaking trumpets to make their voices carry over the roar of the flames. (Author's collection)

to water outlets, and the water turned on. Unfortunately, *America* was a hose cart and could not throw water any great distance, while *Little Giant* was eleven years old (the oldest engine in service). Their limited range forced firefighters to stand very close to the flames. The newer, more powerful pumping engines were either a mile away searching for a phantom fire, or still in their stations.

"The fire was under full headway . . . before the engines arrived, and what could be done?" Chamberlin noted with concern. "Streams were thrown into the flame, and evaporated almost as soon as they struck it. A single fire engine in the blazing forests of Wisconsin would have been as effective as were these machines in [this] forest of shanties. . . ."

The fire had begun near the corner of De Koven and Jefferson and quickly fanned out thanks to increasingly gusty winds. One tongue traveled north up Jefferson, while the other headed east toward Lake Michigan. There was no way firefighters from two engines could contain a wind-driven fire with such a wide front. Still, they did their best.

Two men hauled the cumbersome canvas hose as close to the flames as possible and aimed a stream of water at the burning building. The water hissed and boiled when it struck the burning wood, sending up a vapor of white steam. The firefighters held their position until the fierce heat began to singe the hair on their heads and arms, and their clothes began to smolder. When the pain became unbearable, they staggered back from the flames for a moment's relief, then lunged forward again.

Chamberlin was unimpressed by the efforts of the firefighters he encountered. Many of them were Irish and lived in the surrounding neighborhood, which to some marked them as both ignorant and incompetent. Chamberlin, for instance, felt: "The firemen kept at work fighting the flames — stupidly and listlessly, for they had worked hard all of Saturday night and most of Sunday, and had been enervated by the whisky, which is always copiously poured on such occasions."

That the firefighters had worked through the night and were indeed exhausted was true. And some had celebrated the victory over the previous night's blaze with whisky and beer; though, after sixteen hours of fighting a fire, most simply wanted a soft bed and rest.

More engines began arriving at the scene, as did the department's Chief Marshal Robert A. Williams. A common fire-fighting technique of the time was to surround a blaze with engines and use a flood of water to stop it from spreading. Williams immediately set about repositioning engines, hoping to halt the fire's advance until all the missing equipment could get to the scene.

When the engines and hoses were where he wanted them, Williams turned to one crew and said, "Now, hang on to her here!"

The firefighters were already engulfed in a wave of withering heat, and the flames were reaching out toward them. "Marshal," one of the men yelled, "I don't believe we can stand it here!"

"Stand it as long as you can," Williams told them, before hurrying to another engine. Along the way he noticed that several houses were smoking and on the verge of igniting.

He came upon the driver of *America* and its foreman, John Dorsey. "Turn in a second alarm!" Williams ordered Dorsey. "This is going to spread!" A second alarm would bring in additional engines and men.

Meanwhile, Chamberlin had retreated several blocks in the face of the advancing flames. "I stepped in among some sheds south of Ewing Street; a fence by my side began to blaze; I beat a hasty retreat, and in five minutes the place where I had stood was all ablaze. Nothing could stop that conflagration there. It must sweep on until it reached a broad street, and then, everybody said, it would burn itself out."

The heat and dry air had left twelve-year-old Claire Innes tired and listless all day. She went to bed sometime between eight and eight-thirty only to be startled awake later when a horse-and-

People trapped in burning buildings often panicked and jumped to their deaths. Here two children have been bundled securely in bedding to cushion their fall.

It's possible that the noise that woke Claire Innes was made by a steam engine heading toward the fire. (Author's collection)

wagon clattered past her window at high speed. This was followed by loud voices from the street below her window.

"I was only half awake and not inclined to get up when I heard a man outside say that a fire was burning in the West Division. Father went to the door and asked about the fire and the man repeated what he had told his companions, but this time he added that the fire was a big one and that they were going to have a look at it. Father came inside and said something to Mother. . . . His voice did not sound unusual, [so] I turned over and closed my eyes again."

Claire and her family were staying in the South Division of the city, many blocks from the fire. There really was no reason for them to become alarmed. In fact, most citizens would see the glowing nighttime sky and dismiss it as nothing important. Not even the warning words in that day's *Chicago Tribune* drew much attention: "For days past alarm has followed alarm, but the comparatively trifling losses have familiarized us to the pealing of the Courthouse bell, and we [have] forgotten that the absence of rain for three weeks [has] left everything in so dry and inflammable a condition that a spark might set a fire which would sweep from end to end of the city."

But no one seemed very concerned. This was evident by what Alfred L. Sewell observed while strolling through the city at around 9:30 that night. "Many people were just returning from the Sunday evening services at the various churches when the general alarm was given, but, beyond the immediate vicinity of the beginning of the conflagration, no unusual fear or solicitude was felt by the citizens. The German beerhouses were filled with merry crowds, and as it was a warm evening, the streets all over the city were filled with joyful idlers and promenaders, in their Sunday apparel. A pleasanter, quieter, or a happier evening than was that one is seldom known in a great city."

And despite his own paper's editorial, not even the editor in chief of the *Chicago Tribune,* Horace White, smelled a good story in the smoke that was blowing into his neighborhood. "I had retired to rest, though not to sleep [that night], when the great bell struck the alarm; but fires had been so frequent of late, and had been so speedily extinguished, that I did not deem it worthwhile to get up and look at it, or even to count the strokes of the bell to learn where it was."

As the rest of the city went about its business, fireman Dorsey was racing through the streets to the closest signal box, which happened to be at Goll's drugstore. He opened the small door on the box and used his thumb to pull down the lever. Dorsey then headed back to the scene of the fire, not realizing that he'd made a mistake — he had forgotten to pull down the lever four times, a special signal that would have made it a true second alarm. At the Courthouse, Schaffer and Brown would hear Dorsey's alarm, but, assuming it was simply another signal telling them about the original fire, they failed to call out more engines. The fire had now been burning for over an hour, and the wind was increasing in velocity.

Despite this, Chief Marshal Williams had managed to get a thin circle of engines around the fire. He had five steamers at the scene now, plus three hose carts and a hook-and-ladder wagon, all of them pumping water into the fire at various locations. Spectators were asked to help and many responded by chopping up fences and sidewalks, hoping to deprive the fire of fuel.

One onlooker was a former alderman, James H. Hildreth. Hildreth was the sort of person who liked to get involved in whatever was taking place. The first thing he did was tell Williams that the fire was getting out of control, something Williams could see for himself. Next, he suggested that a firebreak could be created to contain the flames if several houses were blown up, thus depriving the fire of fuel. Williams protested that he did not have the authority or powder to carry out such a drastic plan, but Hildreth persisted, saying he knew where he could get the necessary explosives. Finally, Williams (probably to get the man out of his hair) told him to get the powder.

Meanwhile the heat was beginning to wear down some of the firemen. Charles Anderson remembered when his friend Charles McConners came by and said, "Charley, this is hot!"

"It is, Mac," Anderson replied.

His friend disappeared for a few moments, then returned carrying a wooden door, which he positioned like a warrior's shield between Anderson and the fire.

I have it now, Anderson thought. I can stand it a considerable time.

Anderson no sooner thought this when the door caught fire and burned McConners' hand. McConners flung the door down and then Anderson's clothes began to smoke. The heat was so intense that his leather hat began to twist out of shape.

Williams came by and issued new orders. "Charley, come out as fast as possible. Wet the other side of the street or it will burn!"

Not only was the fire's heat burning the firefighters, it was also creating a powerful updraft that sucked flaming embers and pieces of cloth and wood into the air. One man remembered seeing a

The sky swirls with smoke and flames as building after building catches fire and burns. Two fire engines can be seen throwing thin streams of water at the Tremont House while patrons desperately toss possessions to the ground below. (Frank Leslie's *Illustrated Newspaper*, October 28, 1871)

man's burning shirt sail into the sky, its sleeves outstretched. The wind, which was also increasing in power, took all of these burning objects and blew them over the heads of the firefighters. Spectators tried to stamp out the fires that ignited, but it was clear that a drenching with water was needed desperately.

With the help of onlookers, Anderson began to reposition his

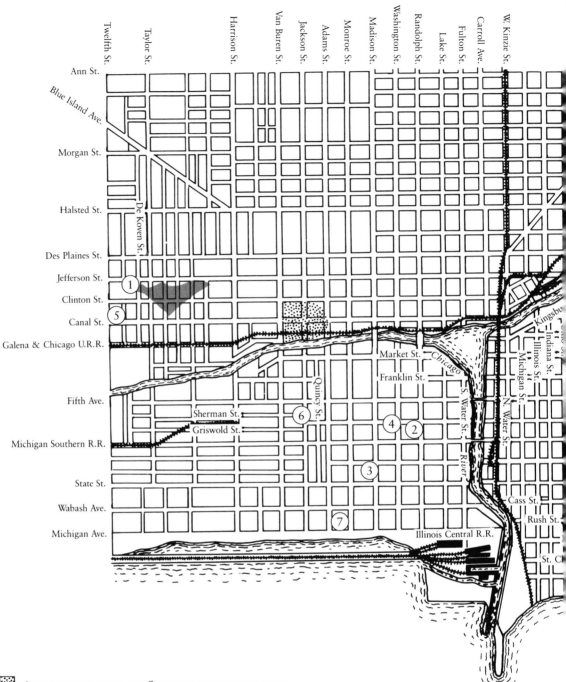

Ann St.

Blue Island Ave.

Morgan St.

Halsted St.

Des Plaines St.

Jefferson St.

Clinton St.

Canal St.

Galena & Chicago U.R.R.

Fifth Ave.

Michigan Southern R.R.

State St.

Wabash Ave.

Michigan Ave.

Twelfth St.

Taylor St.

De Koven St.

Harrison St.

Van Buren St.

Jackson St.

Adams St.

Monroe St.

Madison St.

Washington St.

Randolph St.

Lake St.

Fulton St.

Carroll Ave.

W. Kinzie St.

Kingsbu

Ohio St.

Indiana St.

Illinois St.

Michigan St.

N. Water St.

Chicago River

S. Water St.

Market St.

Franklin St.

Quincy St.

Sherman St.

Griswold St.

Cass St.

Rush St.

Illinois Central R.R.

St. C

AREA DESTROYED BY SATURDAY NIGHT'S FIRE

GRAY AREA INDICATES THE SPREAD OF THE GREAT FIRE

1. Home of Patrick and Catherine O'Leary
2. Courthouse
3. *Tribune* Building
4. Chamber of Commerce Building
5. Bruno Goll's drugstore
6. Neighborhood where Claire Innes and her family lived
7. Horace White's house

Milwaukee Ave.

Division St.

North Ave.

Clybourne Ave.

North Branch, Chicago River

North Branch Canal

Water St.

Center St.

Orchard St.

Asylum Pl.

Fullerton Ave.

Grove St.

Larrabee St.

Belden Ave.

Lincoln Ave.

Sedgwick St.

Elm St.

LINCOLN PARK

Wells St.

La Salle St.

N. Clark St.

Maple St.

Dearborn Ave.

CATHOLIC
CEMETERY

Schiller St.

Thorn St.

Cedar St.

Oak St.

Hickory St.

Whitney St.

White St.

Pearsons St.

LAKE MICHIGAN

hose. He hadn't gotten it very far when water pressure suddenly dropped and only a trickle of liquid came from the hose. A powerful steam engine had arrived at the fire and had simply removed Anderson's hose from its water plug. This was routine procedure, done under the assumption that a steamer would always be more effective than a simple hose cart. Sadly, the steamer did not drag its hose to Anderson's position and he had to watch as four or five houses across the street caught fire.

At the same moment that Anderson's hose stopped, another steamer malfunctioned and its water also gave out. A well-aimed rap of a hammer got the engine working again, but then, at about 10:30, an old section of hose burst and the flow of water stopped again. Two valuable links in the chain of defense were gone, and there was nothing to stop the fire in these locations.

Williams rushed to get the water going and to reposition his engines, but it was too late. The wind had pushed the fire past his circle, a wind that was blowing directly toward the heart of the city.

Later at the official inquiry, all of the mistakes and missed chances that occurred in the opening minutes of the fire would be discussed in great detail. As one firefighter later put it, "From the beginning of that fatal fire, everything went wrong!"

3 · "The Dogs of Hell Were Upon the Housetops"

ONCE THE FIRE BROKE through the circle of engines, it pushed out fists of flame that ate up clapboard siding, shingled roofs, fences, trees, outhouses, and chicken coops. Raised wooden sidewalks caught fire and the wind drove the flames along at a brisk pace. The wind and updraft lifted flames hundreds of feet into the sky and created such a bright light that it reminded some people of daylight.

The firefighters fell back to establish a new line against the advancing fire. By this time, a number of police officers had arrived, and they joined firemen and citizen-volunteers in ripping down fences and sheds. The circle of engines around the fire had been broken, but Williams managed to organize the twelve available engines into three groups. They were effective in stopping the fire's spread west, but the wind pushed it north and east relentlessly. Embers of "red snow" were falling everywhere; some landed on St. Paul's Church four blocks behind the firefighters. If the fire established itself on the tall steeple, the wind would spread firebrands over an even larger area.

Crosby's Opera House burns while pedestrians scamper to safety. Just moments before this scene, a restaurant in the opera house was still serving customers. (*Harper's Weekly*, October 28, 1871)

The light from the blaze was finally getting the attention it deserved from Chicago's citizens. Pedestrians on the street stopped to study the glow and speculate on what direction it was traveling; people hung out of their windows and communicated what they saw to those on the street. One of those watching all of this from a distance was William Brown, the fire alarm operator at the Courthouse who had stubbornly refused to correct Schaffer's original signal to Box 342.

After sending that first signal, Brown settled in to view the fire from his high perch. Some time before ten o'clock, he grew nervous about its increasing size and, without Schaffer's permission, turned in a second alarm to bring in reinforcements. Once again, he pulled Box 342 and sent engines off in the wrong direction. At thirty minutes past ten, Brown pulled a third alarm (which would bring every one of the city's remaining fire engines to the scene) — once again on his own initiative and once again for the wrong box. Fortunately, this one did not cause any harm. The glow from the fire was so bright that engine drivers simply headed toward it.

After the flames chased Joseph Chamberlin, forcing him to retreat, he headed north along Jefferson Street. This would be the western border of the Great Fire and, aside from the thick smoke, relatively safe. At Van Buren Street his curiosity got the best of him and he turned east down the lane so that he could face the leading wall of fire.

"A single engine stood on Van Buren Street, doing what seemed to me good service in preventing the fire from eating its way westward, against the wind. . . . Suddenly, the horses were attached to the engine, and as soon as the hose was reeled it disappeared, whirling northward on Jefferson."

Chamberlin and everyone else around him were confused by this action. Without the engine, houses to the west were threatened. "[Then] I caught the words, 'across the river,' uttered doubtingly by a bystander. The words passed from mouth to mouth, and there was universal incredulity, although the suggestion was communicated through the crowd with startling rapidity."

The crowd soon moved to get out of the smoke and to see if the fire really had leaped across the river. "I went with the rest," Chamberlin remembered, "[and] stood on the embankment that had been Canal Street, and perceived, through the clouds of smoke, a bright light across the river. . . ." As had been feared, the steeple of St. Paul's had ignited and was sending a shower of sparks across the river.

Chamberlin wasted no time. He dashed across the Adams Street viaduct and was shocked at what he saw. "The Armory, the Gasworks, 'Conley's Patch,' and Wells Street as far north as Monroe were all on fire. The wind had increased to a tempest, and hurled great blazing brands over our heads."

Directly east of Chamberlin, and over a mile away, Horace White had been lying in bed for some time when he heard a new set of alarms ringing. It was the general alarm, he recalled, "which distinguishes a great fire from a small one. When it sounded . . . I rose and looked out. There was a great light to the southwest of my residence, but no greater than I had frequently seen in that quarter. . . ."

Grain elevators on the Chicago River are gobbled up, and the masts of the sailing ship in the center have just caught fire. (Harper's Weekly, November 4, 1871)

White was still unconcerned and stayed at his window several minutes more as the distant sky got brighter and brighter. Suddenly, "red tongues of light began to shoot upward."

White dressed hastily, made sure everyone in his family was alerted, then left to go to the *Tribune* office. He planned to write a brief story about this new fire, then go home to get some rest. But "once out upon the street, the magnitude of the fire was suddenly disclosed to me."

What White discovered was that the fire was spreading so rapidly that it was only about five blocks away from his home. "The dogs of hell were upon the housetops," he said, this time with real concern, "bounding from one to another. The fire was moving . . . like an ocean surf on a sand beach. It had already traveled an eighth of a mile and was far beyond control. A column of flame would shoot up from a burning building, catch the force of the wind, and strike the next one, which in turn would perform the same direful office for its neighbor. It was simply indescribable in its terrible grandeur."

At about the same time, Alexander Frear, a New Yorker who was in Chicago visiting his sister-in-law, was leaving the Sherman House and crossing the square where the Courthouse stood. He had overheard people in the hotel corridor talking about a fire, but paid little attention to it since the subject "did not interest me." Outside, he saw the fire's glare, but "thought nothing of it" even though his sister-in-law lived in that direction. What he did notice was that there were few people out, and those he came upon seemed perfectly calm. Out of curiosity he decided to check out the fire before heading to his sister-in-law's house for the night.

When he passed the Methodist church, he heard the congregation singing a joyful hymn. One thing did strike him as unusual. "When I came [outside] the wind was blowing fiercely through Clark Street to the river, and I had some difficulty in getting across the Courthouse square."

Still, Frear ambled on, head bent against the strong wind. It wasn't until he came to a group of men on a corner that he sensed this fire might be different from the previous night's. He asked them what they knew about the fire, "and one of them said, 'It must be a damn big fire this time; you can't put out a high wind

When Alexander Frear left the Sherman House at ten o'clock, the streets were quiet and nearly empty. Several hours later the streets were jammed with frightened people and animals all trying to flee along a narrow street. In the foreground near the center, a little girl has tripped and is falling though no one has noticed. (Chicago Historical Society)

with water.' The rest of them said nothing, but I thought they looked a little scared."

Frear pushed on, quickening his pace. For the first time, he realized that "a great many people were looking out of their windows, and the streets seemed to get full of people suddenly. They were not excited. They stood about in groups listening to the wind, that was making a noise very much like the lake on a stormy night."

At a saloon, Frear stopped to buy a cigar. He was surprised to discover the place completely empty; everyone was out in the street watching the fire's ominous glow. He took a cigar, leaving payment on the bar, and went to light it on a gas burner. Throughout his walk, Frear had maintained his composure, walking calmly and studying faces carefully. "[But] when I was holding [the cigar] up to the gas jet I noticed for the first time that I was considerably excited myself; my hand shook and I could hear my heart beat. I don't think I was two minutes in the place, but when I came out the cinders were falling like snowflakes in every direction and lit the street, and there was a great hubbub of men and vehicles."

Had his sister-in-law's home been in the path of the fire? he wondered. Were she and her children safe? Frear continued his journey, this time running as fast as he could.

In another part of the city, a pounding on her door and calls to get dressed as quickly as possible woke Claire Innes. It was the fire, her mother told her. It had gotten across the river and was coming toward them. "I could hear other voices outside shouting the same thing, so I went to the window. It was very bright on the street, though not as bright as at noontime as some have said. There were people every where, some going toward the fire for a better view, others away from it. A cart was stationed in front of a house and I could see the family — father, mother and children — loading it with furniture, bags and bundles [of clothes] and the like. I dressed and went downstairs where my family was waiting."

Besides her parents, Claire had two brothers and a sister, all of

them younger than she. Evidently, clothes and possibly food had been collected and tossed into tablecloths because Claire then says, "We all took a bundle and left the house, which Father bolted as he would if we were going on a picnic. There was fire to the West and in places it had gotten behind the house as well, though it was still at a distance."

It seems that Claire's family had not been in Chicago very long because her father had his wife and children wait while he asked directions from a man and woman who lived down the block. Her father returned a few moments later and got them started on their journey. "We were to find Clark and take that street to the [Chicago] river and a bridge. The river was quite wide there and once we were across we would be safe — or so the good couple had promised."

Judging from Claire's description, the crowds on her street seem to have been reasonably calm and peaceful. Even the family packing to escape did not appear to be in any great hurry. It's possible that the wind had shifted momentarily and Claire's neighbors did not feel in any immediate danger. In other parts of the city, directly in the path of the fire, the scenes were very different.

Joseph Chamberlin witnessed some of the first unpleasantness not long after the fire broke through the circle of engines. "On that night [the street] was crowded with people pouring out of the thickly settled locality . . ., and here the first panic began. The wretched female inhabitants were rushing out almost naked, imploring spectators to help them on with their burdens of bed quilts, cane-bottomed chairs, iron kettles, etc. Drays were thundering along in the single procession which the narrowness of the street allowed, and all was confusion."

Newspapers of the time loved to add melodramatic touches to their illustrations to heighten the drama of a scene. In this one, two young girls have come upon the body of another girl who was killed when a building collapsed. (Frank Leslie's Illustrated Newspaper, October 28, 1871)

Later Chamberlin passed a lot where people of the "better class" had sought safety. "Two boys, themselves intoxicated, reeled about, each bearing a small cask of whisky out of which he insisted upon treating everyone he met. Soon more casks of whisky appeared, and scores of excited men drank deeply of their contents. The result was, of course, that an equal number of drunken men were soon impeding the flight of the fugitives."

Alexander Frear experienced much the same in his part of the city. He had run several blocks toward his sister-in-law's when he came to a place where the sidewalk was jammed with people. He tried to push his way through the bodies, and when that didn't work, he leaped from the elevated walkway to the street.

Here, horse-drawn wagons and pedestrians vied for space, but were at least moving along slowly. At one spot, Frear saw a man on top of a four-story building shouting something to a man in a third-story window, and this man passed the message to those in the street. "All I could distinctly hear," Frear recalled, "was 'burning on both sides of the river,' and just then there was a great pressure in the crowd of the people and a man on horseback forced his way through. . . . He had in his hand one of those little red flags that switchmen use, which he waved on either side. What he said I could not hear, but it had the effect of producing a panic in the throng."

Frear realized it would be impossible to reach his sister-in-law by a direct route, so he decided to circle back the way he came and search for another way. "No sooner had I turned around, than I saw the light of the fire extending far back in the direction I had come, the flames lighting the houses on the east side of Clark Street as far as I could see. . . ."

Frear had no choice but to follow the movement of the crowd as it struggled to find a path not yet blocked by smoke and fire.

Claire and her family made their way to Clark Street and headed toward the bridge. "Father was very upset and several times told us to stay close together and to hurry along."

Even if an individual managed to get his or her possessions on a wagon that did not mean they were going to be saved. Artist Alfred R. Waud has captured this wagon in full flight just as its contents have caught fire. (Chicago Historical Society)

As the fire ate its way through the city, thousands of people were made homeless. This group has escaped the flames, though a new realization has begun to set in: Everything they worked for and owned is gone. (Chicago Historical Society)

State Street was much busier than the side street where they lived. The sidewalks were crowded with people; the foolhardy and curious stood in clumps watching the advancing flames, while others hurried along to escape them. Wagons clogged the streets and the frantic shouts of the drivers added to the confusion and sense of panic.

"We went two or three blocks, I don't remember exactly how many . . . when movement became impossible. [My brother] Willy dropped his bundle and became upset when he could not find it again. Sparks and cinders now began to fall all around us and I saw a window awning of a house catch fire. . . . Ahead of us there was much shouting and then the crowd began to push back on us. Father told us to drop our bundles and hold hands, but I did not drop mine. The crowd moved forward a little, then people began turning and pushing against us. There was no resisting the crush and we were swept along. I turned around at some point and saw a building burst into flames as if it were built of dry straw."

AREA DESTROYED BY SATURDAY NIGHT'S FIRE

GRAY AREA INDICATES THE SPREAD OF THE GREAT FIRE

1. Home of Patrick and Catherine O'Leary
2. Courthouse
3. *Tribune* Building
4. Chamber of Commerce Building
5. Bruno Goll's drugstore
6. Neighborhood where Claire Innes and her family lived
7. Horace White's house

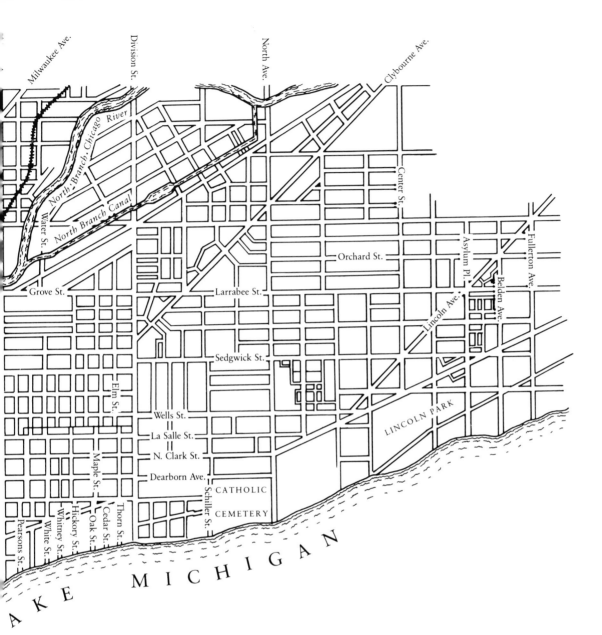

8. St. Paul's Church
9. Armory
10. Gasworks
11. "Conley's Patch"
12. Sherman House
13. Tremont House
14. Crosby's Opera House
15. Grain elevator
16. Home of Alexander Frear's sister

57

4 · "A Surging Ocean of Flame"

DESPITE ROUGH SHOVING and bumping, Claire managed to cling to her bundle and stay right behind the rest of her family. Others weren't so lucky. In the rush and panic, a number of people either lost their footing or were accidentally pushed from the sidewalk and into the busy street. Frantic animals — stray horses and cows, dogs and cats, and even rats — ran wild, causing increasingly more confusion.

"The retreat was now a stampede and we were swept along," a frightened Claire recalled. "I felt as a leaf . . . in a great rushing river. We turned up a street of bookshops, some of which had had their windows broken. Father picked up Willy and was carrying him, while Mother held Charlotte and Robert by the hand. I was some steps behind. The wind was terrible, like a storm, and filled with cinders and fire. I held up my hand to keep them from my eyes."

Claire and her family continued down the street when "a short, rough man grabbed at my bundle [but I] would not let it go. I called for Father and almost lost my bundle except that another

The very sturdy-looking Chamber of Commerce Building has ignited and a rain of fiery embers falls on the people below. (Harper's Weekly, October 28, 1871)

man took hold of [the man] and dragged him away. When I turned, I could not find Father or Mother or my sister or brothers. I ran down the sidewalk after them, calling their names and searching everywhere for a familiar face. They were gone — into the smoke and dark and falling fire. I stood near a corner hoping Father or Mother would return for me, and would have stayed there throughout the night, except that a building up the street began to burn, and then the roof of another and the mob came back at me and I was once again forced to move."

Claire and the charging crowd went back up the street. At some point, Claire edged herself toward the shops and leaped into a tiny alleyway between two buildings. She probably hoped that by standing there she might catch a glimpse of her family hurrying past. "I looked at every face, but I could not find them. When everyone had gone by, I stood in the middle of the sidewalk and shouted for them. It was no use. Except for a few [people] still observing the fire's approach or dragging their possessions to safety, I was alone on the street, and you can imagine what I must have felt."

Claire wasn't the only one to witness mass panic. The wind had increased in velocity, and burning chunks of wood were being carried for many blocks before they fell to earth. No accurate measure of the wind's velocity was made during the fire, though many eyewitnesses claimed it was as strong as a hurricane. It's likely that the wind was blowing at a steady 30 miles per hour with some ferocious gusts. The stronger winds, the ones people remembered the best, were probably caused by rising convective heat.

As the fire burned and heated up an area (sometimes to 1500 degrees), the hot air rose and formed a column hundreds of feet tall. Oxygen-rich air was sucked into the column at the base, where it mixed with the burning fuels and also rose, twisting and whirling around as it did. Sometimes giant bubbles of unburned gases rose within the column and then exploded high in the sky. The wind generated from such a column could reach out hundreds of feet and might attain hurricanelike speeds.

At its fiercest, such a whirlwind could rip a roof off a house and pick up the building's contents. In addition, many people had hauled furniture from burning buildings and abandoned it in the streets in hopes of saving it. Burning mattresses and dressers were scooped up by the furious gale and hurled hundreds of feet. A block that was safe and fire free one moment, might burst into flames a second later. Thousands of people found themselves surrounded by flames and smoke and rushing headlong to escape.

Reporter Joseph Chamberlin spent hours roaming the streets, often finding himself dodging showers of scorching sparks. At one point the heat became too intense, so he ducked into an abandoned store where he found a large blanket on the floor. Wrapping it around his head and body, he ventured out into the street again and made his way to the leading edge of the fire, which had reached the intersection of Franklin and Randolph.

A crush of pushing, shoving, and panic-stricken people dash across the Randolph Street Bridge. This picture was drawn when the fire was several blocks away, which is why empty wagons are heading back for more loads, and spectators along the shore are still taking in the show. (Author's collection)

"And now the scene of confusion had reached its height," Chamberlin observed through the folds of the blanket. "Wagons were rushing through the streets laden with stocks of goods, books, valuable papers, boxes of money, and everything conceivable; scores of men were dragging trunks frantically along the sidewalks, knocking down women and children; fabulous sums of money were offered truckmen for conveyances."

The fire advanced, forcing Chamberlin to flee up Randolph toward a bridge. "The noise of the conflagration was terrific. To the roar which the simple process of combustion always makes, magnified here to so grand an extent, was added the crash of falling buildings and the constant explosions of stores of oil and other like material. The noise of the crowd was nothing compared with this chaos of sound. All these things — the great, dazzling, mounting light, the crash and roar of the conflagration, and the desperate flight of the crowd — combined to make a scene of which no intelligent idea can be conveyed in words."

An exhausted Chamberlin came to the Randolph Street Bridge and discovered "a torrent of humanity pouring over the bridge. The Madison street bridge had long before become impassable, and Randolph was the only outlet for the entire region south of it. Drays, express wagons, trucks, and conveyances of every conceivable species and size crowded across in indiscriminate haste. Collisions happened almost every moment, and when one overloaded wagon broke down, there were enough men on hand to drag it and its contents over the bridge by force."

Chamberlin was too tired to fight his way across just then, so he crawled up onto one of the bridge's arched railings. From this high perch, the reporter spotted an undertaker struggling to get his supply of coffins to safety. "He had taken a dray, but was unable to load all of his goods into the vehicle, so he employed half a dozen boys, gave each of them a coffin, took a large one himself, and headed the weird procession. The sight of those coffins, upright, and bobbing along just above the heads of the crowd . . . was somewhat startling and the unavoidable suggestion was that they were escaping across the river to be ready for use when the debris of the conflagration should be cleared away."

The fire seemed to pour down Randolph Street, gobbling up building after building. Despite the fire's approach, the heat and shower of burning debris, Chamberlin remained calm, watching the dramatic scene in front of him and mentally taking notes. Then suddenly "the fire was a mountain over our heads. The barrels of oil in Heath's store exploded with a sound like rattling musketry. The great north wall of the Nevada Hotel plunged inward with hardly a sound, so great was the din of the surrounding conflagration. The Garden City House burned like a box of matches. . . . Toward the east and northeast we looked upon a surging ocean of flame."

With the air now scorching hot, Chamberlin did what he should have done in the first place. He slid off the railing and joined the terrified crowd pushing and shoving its way to safety.

Alexander Frear's experiences in the fire were, if anything, even more horrifying. After being forced back by the fire earlier, he went north and circled all the way around it until he located his sister-in-law's house on Des Plaines Street. The house was just one block from Jefferson Street, where the fire still raged. Because the heat was incredible and the wind was threatening to blow the fire in their direction, everyone on the block was preparing to flee.

Frear's first job was to get the three children to safety, one of whom was an invalid. While his sister-in-law and a friend of the family, Mr. Wood, continued to pack, Frear got the children into a wagon and took them to another friend's house ten blocks away (and presumably well out of the path of the fire). On the return trip, he came to a bridge that had opened to let boats sail downriver and away from the burning areas. "It seemed that the string of vessels passing through was endless," an impatient Frear remembered. "[I was] an hour and a half in getting back, I think. The whole of Ewing Street was barricaded with vehicles and household effects."

A few minutes after he got back to his sister-in-law's, Mr. Wood

Hundreds of people found themselves surrounded by fire and fled to the Government Pier, only to be trapped there. The fire would nibble at the pier, but frantic work — and the fact that water was readily available — enabled citizens to halt the advancing flames. (The Illustrated London News, October 28, 1871)

appeared suddenly. [He] burst into the room. . . . His appearance as well as his language was terrifying. Nearly blinded by the flying embers he had dashed water on his head and face, and his matted hair and begrimed skin added to his frightened looks made him seem like another person."

Mr. Wood's message was even more upsetting — the fire had leaped forward and was threatening the block where the children were staying.

Frear, his sister-in-law, and Mr. Wood fought their way down the street, jumped into a horse-drawn cab, and set out to find the children. Most streets in the immediate vicinity of the fire were impassable due to the crowds of people or abandoned furniture. Once again, Frear had to head north, well out of his way, before he could work his way close to his destination.

"We got as far as Washington Street in the avenue when [we were] stopped and got into an altercation with an officer. . . . I sprang out and was told that it was useless to go any farther, for the whole of the avenue was on fire. The roadway was full of people, and the din of voices and the melee of horses rendered unmanageable by the falling embers was terrible."

Frear learned that the block they were looking for was burning. "To add to my distress, Mrs. Frear jumped out of the vehicle and started to run in the direction of the fire. Nothing . . . saved her from being crushed to death in a mad attempt to find her children but the providential appearance of an acquaintance, who told her that the children were all safe at the St. James Hotel."

They dashed to the St. James and made a frantic search for the children. They were not in the building. Wondering if the acquaintance had gotten the name of the hotel wrong, Frear left his sister-in-law and Wood at the St. James and ran three blocks to another large hotel, the Sherman House.

The scene there was one of wild disorder and panic. The roof had caught fire in several places and while the flames had been extinguished, smoke was still oozing down the stairways and along the halls. Frear reached the top floor and began searching each room. "The corridor was a scene of intense excitement. The guests of the house were running about wildly, some of them dragging their trunks to the stairway. Everything was in confusion, and my heart sank within me as I saw the panic spreading. . . ."

He did not find the children there either, but he did happen to bump into another nephew. They decided to team up in the search and go to other nearby hotels.

The two had only gone two blocks when they found themselves exhausted and thirsty. Fortunately, Wright's Restaurant was still open, so they ducked in for "a drink of coffee, which I needed

Many stories circulated about vigilante justice dispensed during the fire, such as the hanging of arsonists. (Chicago Historical Society)

very much. There were several of the firemen of the *Little Giant* in there. One of the men was bathing his head with whisky from a flask. They declared that the entire [fire] department had given up, overworked, and that they could do nothing more."

This wasn't exactly accurate. Much of the fire department was still at work, even though they knew the fire was completely out of control. Engines and men had scattered as the fire advanced and were now operating on their own, essentially trying to save individual buildings here and there. Chief Marshal Williams, for instance, had jumped aboard a passing engine and was now at one of the remaining bridge crossings, hosing it down.

In another section of the city, James Hildreth had gotten hold of 2,500 pounds of explosives and was setting off charges to create a firebreak. His first few attempts were dismal failures. He had underestimated the powder needed to level the structures and managed only to blow out windows and an occasional wall (which opened the buildings up to the fire). But there were still thousands of buildings in the path of the fire, and Hildreth had lots of powder and energy. He wasn't the sort of man who gave up easily either; it might take a few more attempts, but he knew he'd get the hang of it eventually.

Of course, Alexander Frear wasn't aware of any of this just then. He and his nephew were drinking their coffee when "an Irish girl was brought in with her dress nearly all burnt from her person. It had caught on the Courthouse steps from a cinder." After viewing this scene, Frear and his nephew left the restaurant and hurried off quickly to search for his sister-in-law's children.

"We passed a broken-down steamer in the middle of the roadway. The avenue was a scene of desolation. The storm of falling fire seemed to increase every second. . . . Looking back . . . toward the Opera House, I saw the smoke and flames pouring out of State Street, from the very point we had just left, and the intervening space was filled with the whirling embers that beat against the houses and covered the roofs and windowsills."

The wind-driven fire was actually moving faster than Frear and his nephew, and had swept past them in places. "To add to the terrors, the animals, burnt and infuriated by the cinders, darted through the streets regardless of all human obstacles. . . . The flames from the houses on the west side reached in a diagonal arch quite across the street, and occasionally the wind would lift the great body of flame, detach it entirely from the burning buildings, and hurl it with terrific force far ahead."

They had entered an area of large homes, and Frear was shocked to find the same disorder as in the poorer neighborhoods. Frear,

The Courthouse burns while people on the street attempt to save themselves and their possessions. (*Frank Leslie's Illustrated Newspaper*, October 28, 1871)

like many of the wealthier and more educated of the time, viewed the less fortunate as inferior. In an emergency, the poor would panic, become confused and go wild; the "better class" would remain calm and law-abiding, and find an orderly way to deal with the problem. What Frear witnessed was anything but a civilized retreat.

"All the mansions were being emptied with the greatest disorder and the greatest excitement. Nobody endeavored to stay the flames now. A mob of men and women, all screaming and shouting, ran about wildly, crossing each other's paths, and intercepting each other as if deranged. We tried to force our way along the avenue, which was already littered with costly furniture, some of it burning in the streets under the falling sparks, but it was next to impossible. . . . I saw a woman kneeling in the street with a crucifix held up before her and the skirt of her dress burning while she prayed. We had barely passed before a runaway truck dashed her to the ground. Loads of goods passed us . . . that were burning on the trucks, and my nephew says that he distinctly saw one man go up to a pile of costly furniture lying in front of an elegant residence and deliberately hold a piece of burning packing board under it until the pile was lit."

At this point, Frear decided that searching for the children was fruitless. "Mrs. Frear's children had been lost," he concluded. He and his nephew fought their way back to the St. James Hotel to tell his sister-in-law the sad news, only to learn that she and Wood had been moved north to a safer location. Frear and his nephew were trying to get out of the hotel when "word was brought that the bridges were burning, and all escape was cut off to the north and west. . . . Men shouted the news and added to the panic. Women, half-dressed, and many of them with screaming children, fled out of the building. There was a jam in the doorway, and they struck and clawed each other as if in self-defense. I lost sight of my nephew at this time."

He searched the teeming crowd for the young man, but realized spotting him would be impossible. Besides, the fire was closing in

Chicago is blackened and burned, and several ships on Lake Michigan are in flames. The fire would continue to burn until it reached Fullerton Avenue, which is to the right almost two miles from the front wall of the fire shown here. (*Harper's Weekly,* October 28, 1871)

again. On his own now, Frear ran for his life, going up any street that was not consumed in flames. In the business district, he saw looters piling wagons high with all sorts of goods. On another street, he passed a boy who had been killed by a piece of marble thrown from a window. "One little girl, in particular, I saw, whose golden hair was loose down her back and caught afire. She ran screaming past me, and somebody threw a glass of liquor upon her, which flared up and covered her with a blue flame."

Luckily for Frear, the report that all bridges had been destroyed wasn't absolutely true. He came upon one that was severely damaged, but still sturdy enough to bear the load of the fleeing mob. "The rail of the bridge was broken away, and a number of small boats loaded with goods were passing down the stream. How many people were pushed over the bridge into the water I cannot tell. I myself saw one man stumble under a load of clothing and disappear; nor did the occupants of the boats pay the slightest attention to him nor to the crowd overhead, except to guard against anybody falling into their vessels."

Frear got across the river "after a severe struggle, and at the risk of my life" and continued his search for his sister-in-law and Wood. Minutes after his crossing, the bridge caught fire again, only this time, the flames could not be put out. The tar-saturated wood burned like a torch, crackling wildly as the fire inched across the structure as if it were stalking another victim. Bits of burning debris fell from the bridge and set boats below on fire. Eventually, the bridge collapsed under its own weight and plunged into the water with a hissing roar.

Claire Innes, Joseph Chamberlin, and Alexander Frear had all seen mass panic, crime, and acts of violence. Others, such as Horace White, were much more fortunate.

White's trip to the *Tribune* offices was relatively easy. He discovered a number of workers from the editorial and composing rooms still in the building. A few were rushing to get out a special edition about the fire, while the rest were on the roof hosing it down with water.

The *Tribune* Building was one of the newer "fireproof" structures, one which, for many citizens, symbolized the wealth and energy of Chicago. In addition to a granite-block exterior, the interior ceilings were of corrugated iron, resting upon wrought iron I beams, and every partition wall in the structure was of brick. It was, in all respects, one of the most absolutely fireproof buildings ever erected. That is, in every respect but one — the roof. The roof was a typical tar-over-wood affair, which meant, in addition to keeping it wet, the men on it were constantly dancing around to stamp out burning cinders.

Editor White watched from an upper floor as the fire marched down the block toward the *Tribune* Building. His tone had a victorious ring to it as he described what happened. "We saw the tall buildings on the opposite sides of the two streets melt down in a few moments without scorching ours. The heat broke the plate-glass windows in the lower stories, but not the upper ones. After the fire in our neighborhood had spent its force, the editorial and composing rooms did not even smell of smoke."

White surveyed the terrain around the building and was able to pick out several other fireproof buildings, each of which had not only resisted the fire, but seemed to have stopped its relentless advance. When White left the *Tribune* offices, fires were burning on all sides, but, aside from blackened scorch marks, his building stood tall and proud. As he hurried home, White felt triumphant, "supposing that all danger to [the *Tribune* Building] had passed."

White did not realize it at the time, but the *Tribune* Building and all other fireproof structures had another fatal flaw. Their water supplies. As he later admitted, "I did not reflect that the city Waterworks, with their four great pumping engines, were in a straight line with the fire and wind. Nor did I know then that this priceless machinery was covered by a wooden roof. The flames were driving thither with demon precision."

When the Waterworks burned down at around three in the morning, the pumping machines went dead, and the water supply to the city stopped. The men at the *Tribune* would do their best to stamp out and smother the burning embers that landed on the roof, but eventually, the fire won out. The shock felt by White and other citizens when they learned the *Tribune* was a gutted skeleton was captured perfectly by Charles Mackintosh. After describing at great length how solid and fireproof the *Tribune* Building was, Mackintosh paused and, with a sad sigh, he concluded, "That is, it was fireproof up to the date of its destruction."

Back at home, White and his family struggled to pile "seven trunks, four bundles, four valises, two baskets, and one hamper of provisions" onto a wagon. Leaving his family behind to pack up his library, White grabbed a birdcage "containing a talented

The Chicago Tribune *Building would hold off the devouring flames much longer than most buildings. Eventually, its weaknesses of construction, plus a lack of water, would lead to its destruction.* (Author's collection)

green parrot" and drove toward a friend's house where he hoped to store his possessions.

"The dust was so thick that we could not see the distance of a whole square ahead. It came, not in clouds, but in a steady storm of sand, the particles impinging against our faces like needle points. Pretty soon we came to a dead halt. We could move neither forward, nor backward, nor sidewise. The gorge had caught fast somewhere."

The fire was only about a quarter of a mile from White's wagon and was moving closer. But White and the others in the area were in luck, at least for the moment. The wind had shifted, slowing the march of the flames eastward and giving them precious minutes to untangle the traffic jam.

With the danger lessened, White did not experience the terror or panic that others did. " . . . Everybody was good-natured and polite. If I should say I didn't hear an oath all the way down Michigan Avenue, there are probably some mule drivers in Cincinnati who would say it was a lie. But I did not. . . . There was no panic, no frenzy, no boisterousness, but only the haste which the situation authorized."

Eventually, White got his wagon through, deposited his possessions, and headed back. On the way, he came upon his family, "their arms full of light household effects. My wife told me that the house was already burned, that the flames burst out ready-made in the rear hall before she knew that the roof had been scorched. . . ."

White turned the wagon around and again headed south, his family and all of his servants safely onboard.

Like many other Chicagoans, especially those with strong economic interests in the city, White would steadfastly refuse to believe that a significant number of people had panicked, rioted, or engaged in any sort of criminal acts. After all, a city that had gone wild would not instill much confidence in potential business investors. Oh, there had been some trouble, they would admit, but it was caused by the lowest sort of people, the same ones who were the cause of the fire. For the most part, White and others insisted, Chicago had remained civilized and orderly.

"I saw a great many kindly acts done as we moved along," White would recall almost fondly. "The poor helped the rich, and the rich helped the poor (if anybody could be called rich at such a time) to get on with their loads. I heard of cartmen demanding one hundred and fifty dollars (in hand, of course) for carrying a single load. Very likely it was so, but those cases did not come under my own notice. It did come under my notice that some cartmen worked for whatever the sufferers felt able to pay, and one I knew worked with alacrity for nothing. It takes all sorts of people to make a great fire."

White's escape took him four miles outside of the city to an unoccupied cottage his brother owned. The fire was miles away to the north, a distant, pulsing red sky. And while White and his family had escaped the fire, the "wind blew with increasing violence, till [the] frame house trembled in every rafter."

White and his family kept an uneasy watch. "The grass was as dry as tinder," he recalled. If the wind should shift, the fire "might invade the South Division itself, and come up under the impulsion of that fierce wind, and where should we all be then?"

The wind did not turn. It continued driving the fire through the heart of Chicago, devouring churches, banks, publishing houses and printers, breweries, grain elevators, lumberyards, and department stores as if they were constructed of brittle hay. Buildings that citizens viewed with great pride, such as the Courthouse, were gobbled up.

After crossing the Chicago River for a second time and invading the North Division, the fire widened its front. Tens of thousands of people scrambled for their lives, became trapped and confused; most figured out how to escape, but scores of people perished in

Once the flames had swept past, the homeless settled in for a night of living on the street. (Harper's Weekly, October 28, 1871)

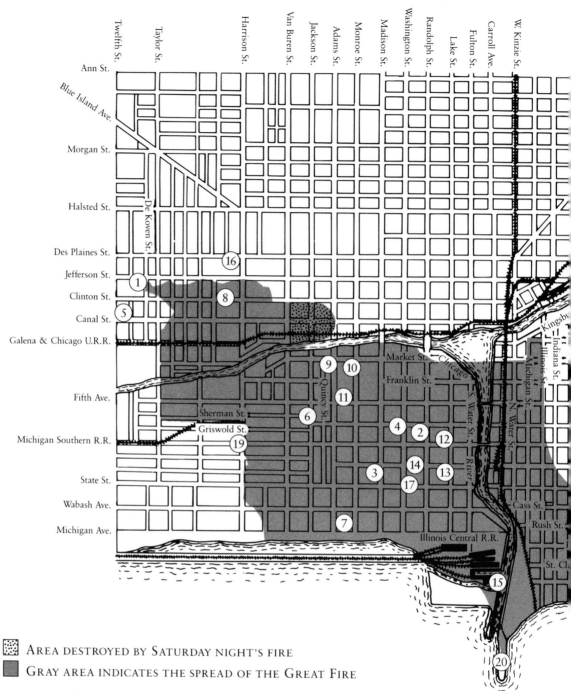

▨ Area destroyed by Saturday night's fire

▣ Gray area indicates the spread of the Great Fire

1. Home of Patrick and Catherine O'Leary
2. Courthouse
3. *Tribune* Building
4. Chamber of Commerce Building
5. Bruno Goll's drugstore
6. Neighborhood where Claire Innes and her family lived
7. Horace White's house
8. St. Paul's Church
9. Armory

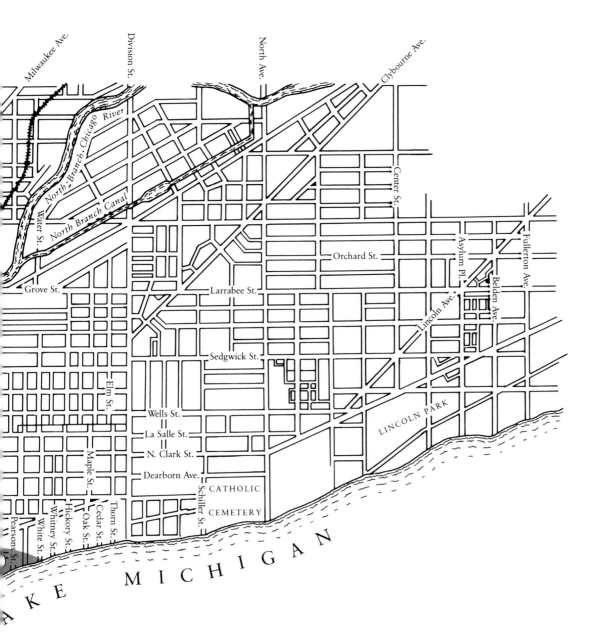

Milwaukee Ave.
Division St.
North Ave.
Clybourne Ave.
North Branch, Chicago River
North Branch Canal
Water St.
Center St.
Asylum Pl.
Fullerton Ave.
Orchard St.
Belden Ave.
Grove St.
Larrabee St.
Lincoln Ave.
Sedgwick St.
LINCOLN PARK
Elm St.
Wells St.
La Salle St.
N. Clark St.
Dearborn Ave.
Maple St.
CATHOLIC
Schiller St.
CEMETERY
Pearsons St.
White St.
Whitney St.
Hickory St.
Cedar St.
Oak St.
Thorn St.

LAKE MICHIGAN

10. Gasworks
11. "Conley's Patch"
12. Sherman House
13. Tremont House
14. Crosby's Opera House
15. Grain elevator
16. Home of Alexander Frear's sister-in-law
17. St. James Hotel
18. Waterworks
19. Area dynamited by James Hildreth
20. Government Pier

dead-end streets. Hundreds of people near the shores of Lake Michigan had no other choice but to wade into the cold water. They would stand there for hours, the water to their shoulders, with a panoramic view of their city in flames.

In the middle of this smoke and fire was Claire Innes. After being separated from her family and failing to locate them in the mob, "I ran up the street after the rest. The fire was everywhere, and the crowd split up, everyone taking the route they thought the safest. I followed the largest number for a block, but they scattered at every alley and turn until I decided to choose my own direction. Fire and smoke and dust were every where, so I ran up a street with the least of them."

At this point in her letter, Claire doesn't detail her every move. In all likelihood, she continued to run in whichever direction seemed the most fire and smoke free. When her letter resumes, she tells us "I was all turned around and more tired than I can ever remember being. I was choking on the smoke and dust and I looked for a quiet place to rest. A little way along I came to a wide alley and went down it to an empty section filled with bricks and boards, barrels and ladders and such."

Claire rested on a barrel, plopping her bundle down beside her. The air was somewhat clearer in the alley, though the choking smell of smoke and wind-driven dust must have been ever present. While she sat there "a man hurried past me without a word, followed by another. A third went by and said something to me over his shoulder, but I did not understand him as he spoke only German. When I looked to where the men had just been, I saw smoke and fire blocking the entrance. I remember feeling very frightened by how quickly the fire had appeared, though this was nothing when compared to how I felt a moment later. I went to follow the men, but they were already gone and the other end of the alley was all fire and smoke, too."

It was as if giant iron gates had crashed shut and bolted themselves. Claire was now locked inside the alley, trapped, with the fire coming at her from all sides.

5 · "Chicago Is in Flames"

Claire wasted little time in being frightened. Her first thought was to see if one or the other of the alley openings might be passable despite the billowing smoke. She got within thirty feet of the thick smoke only to be driven back. "The heat was like that of an oven. I tried to open the door to a building, but found it bolted. Smoke was escaping from under the other doors, so I gave up hope of finding safety through them."

As the roofs and then the interiors of the surrounding structures were consumed by the flames, a scorching wind swept around the alley. The rain of burning embers grew heavier and more unbearable. Claire retreated, seeking the safest, coolest place, and found herself back at the construction site.

"I cannot say I actually decided to hide behind the bricks since I could not hear myself think in the terrible noise. I did not even look at the fire, but hid my face in the dirt and pulled my bundle, which I had retrieved, over my head."

For understandable reasons, Claire did not spend much time observing the burning buildings around her, so her description of what happened is limited. It can be reasonably assumed that she was surrounded by a frightening cacophony of sounds — wood igniting and burning wildly, the glass of windows exploding, stairways and ceilings collapsing. When the interior support framing of a building had been eaten through and weakened enough, parts of the exterior brick walls would fall with a ground-rumbling roar.

The pile of bricks Claire hid behind shielded her from the severest heat and most of the flying debris. But there is little doubt that she had a great deal of luck on her side as well. For one thing, it's likely that most of the building walls did not collapse to release a wave of fire and heat; those walls that did give way, fell far enough from her so that she was not crushed. Other factors may have contributed to her survival. The buildings that ringed the construction site might have had few windows, thus containing the baking heat of their fires to some extent. Most important, a deadly convection column never established itself in the immediate area so a blanket of killing heat and fire did not cover her.

Exactly how long it took for the buildings to burn is not clear; Claire only says that it took "many minutes." It probably took much longer, an hour or more for the fires to completely gut the structures that lined the alley. During all of this time, "[I] kept my head hidden beneath the bundle and said my prayers."

Once the main force of the fire began to lessen, Claire peeked out. What she saw must have astonished her. Sturdy brick structures had been transformed into blackened skeletons whose insides continued to burn brightly. Still, Claire had more immediate concerns.

"My legs and arms and back [were] all burnt where my dress caught fire. . . . I put out the fire and made ready to leave, which was not easy as the [alleyway] openings were blocked with brick and burning wood and smoke. I called [for help] again and again and at last a voice called back to me through the smoke. He told me to stand away from there as a wall of the building might fall on me, and that was all. This made me even more alarmed, but I did not want to stay in the alley alone, so I began climbing. The bricks were still hot — very hot — but I found that if I did not stop [moving] my feet were not burnt so bad."

Claire scrambled over the smoldering pile of debris and made it to the street. She was by no means safe. Buildings up and down the block were burning and collapsing, punctuated every so often by the explosion of flammable liquids. Abandoned pieces of furniture on the street and sidewalk were fiery torches, while shadowy figures darted through the night seeking a safe escape. Claire made her way along the street with single-minded purpose. "Now," she said, sensing the enormity of the task facing her, "I had to find my family in all of this."

During the night, James Hildreth and his men were hard at work trying to prevent the fire from spreading south. After the first few blasts failed to bring down the structures, Hildreth figured out precisely how much powder was needed. Soon he and his helpers were blasting apart house after house along Harrison Street. By the time they had reached the Wabash Avenue Methodist Episcopal Church, they were capable of setting off a powerful charge every five minutes.

With the houses leveled, local residents grabbed buckets and kept the debris soaked until the threat of fire passed. Hildreth's methods appeared harsh to many people, especially to those who saw their homes blown up while the fire was still blocks away. But there is little doubt that the firebreaks he created halted the southward creep of the fire and saved several blocks of homes from destruction.

While the fire was being contained in the south, to the north another story was unfolding. The width and speed of the fire made it impossible for weary firemen to work in an organized or coordinated way. Besides, they were now beyond exhaustion. Two nights of fire fighting and little rest or food had pushed many to the brink of collapse. Several had to be taken from the area in wagons. One tired fireman sat down on a street corner to catch

When Chicago awoke, the center of the city looked as if it had been bombarded by heavy cannons. (Author's collection)

his breath and promptly fell asleep despite the roar of the fire around him.

At six o'clock on Monday morning, the fire had been burning over nine hours, and seemed capable of continuing its march north unless more help could be found. Chicago's mayor, Robert B. Mason, had been up all night receiving reports about the spread of the fire and praying for a miracle. Finally, he gave up hope and sent urgent telegrams to the surrounding cities and towns. "CHICAGO IS IN FLAMES," read his message to the mayor of

Milwaukee. "SEND YOUR WHOLE DEPARTMENT TO HELP US."

Aid came pouring in from Milwaukee, Cincinnati, Dayton, Louisville, Detroit, Port Huron, Bloomington, Springfield, Janesville, Allegheny, and Pittsburgh. Some cities sent steamers and ladder wagons, others sent badly needed hose and fresh firefighters. And many did so at great risk. Milwaukee put three steamers and their crews onboard a train, leaving that city with only one working engine.

The sun rose on Monday, and Chicago continued to burn. The fire went largely unchecked because the additional men and equipment took many hours to arrive.

After narrowly escaping the flames the night before, Joseph Chamberlin had gone to the North Division to watch the fire there. Just before seven o'clock, he went back to the West Division. "Then a curious-looking crimson ball came up out of the lake, which they said was the sun; but oh, how sickly and insignificant it looked! I had watched the greatest of the world's conflagrations from its beginning . . . and although the fire was still blazing all over the city with undiminished luster, I could not look at it. I was almost unable to walk with exhaustion and the effects of a long season of excitement, and sought my home for an hour's sleep."

Chamberlin went up Madison Street into an area untouched by the fire and was startled when he met "scores of working girls on their way 'down town' as usual, bearing their lunch-baskets, as if nothing had happened. They saw the fire and smoke before them, but could not believe that the city, with their means of livelihood, had been swept away during the night."

Because telephones, radios, and televisions did not exist, people in the distant portions of Chicago did not know very much about the fire. Many people had seen the bright glow in the distance, but the true degree of disaster was not known until burned-out friends and relatives began knocking on their doors. Then, telegraph lines hummed with brief accounts of the tragedy, and these details were passed from city to city. Fuller accounts would follow. Before the end of Monday, the Chicago *Evening Journal* managed to get a one-page edition onto the streets. In searing headlines, it announced:

THE GREAT CALAMITY OF THE AGE!

Chicago in Ashes!!

Hundreds of Millions of Dollars' Worth of Property Destroyed

The South, the North and a Portion of the West Divisions of the City in Ruins.

All the Hotels, Banks, Public Buildings, Newspaper Offices and Great Business Blocks Swept Away.

The Conflagration Still in Progress.

Fury of the Flames.

Details, Etc., Etc.

Alexander Frear probably wished he could turn his back on the fire and find a cozy bed. Unfortunately, his adventures with the fire were far from over.

After fleeing across the burning bridge, Frear went directly to where his sister-in-law's house had been, his heart filled with grief. He had long ago decided that her three children had perished in the fire; now, on top of this, he had lost track of his sister-in-law, Mr. Wood, and another nephew in the chaos of the night. He presumed the worst.

He must have been pleasantly shocked not just to discover the house intact, but to be greeted at the door by his nephew and Mr. Wood. What's more, they "informed me that Mrs. Frear had been taken to a private house in Huron Street, and was perfectly safe and well cared for."

At this point, Frear gave in to his physical exhaustion. "I was wet and scorched and bedraggled. My clothes were burnt full of holes on my arms and shoulders and back. . . . I fell down in the hallway and went to sleep."

Less than a half hour later, Frear was shaken awake and told that "Mrs. Frear must be moved again."

Mr. Wood knew exactly where she was on Huron Street, and volunteered to lead Frear there. They went as quickly as possible up Des Plaines Street. For most of the way, houses blocked their view of the burnt and burning section of the city, but when they neared a bridge crossing to the North Division, the view opened up before them.

"It was about eight-thirty o'clock," Frear recalled. "We could see across the river at the cross streets that where yesterday was a populous city was now a mass of smoking ruins. All the way round we encountered thousands of people; but the excitement had given way to a terrible grief and desolation."

For the first time since the start of the fire, the light of day allowed everyone to see and feel the true extent of damage. Alfred Sewell noted the stunned emotions of the vast majority of citizens: "O, what a horrible scene was presented to the view of the

Twisted metal and crumbled brick are all that is left of the Post Office and Custom House. When people saw post-fire photographs, the scenes reminded them of burned-out cities from the Civil War. (Chicago Historical Society)

spectator on that gloomy [morning]. . . . Heaps of ruins, and here and there a standing wall, as far as the eye could reach, and far beyond, for a stretch of four miles. . . . We walked through the streets, covered every-where with heaps of debris and parts of walls, and could not help comparing ourselves to ghosts wandering through a vast grave-yard. 'Am I really awake, or am I having a horrible dream?' is a question we seriously asked ourselves many times. . . ."

People were stunned and overwhelmed, and probably feared the worst about relatives and friends who might have been in the path of the Great Fire. But Frear had to push aside his emotions and exhaustion — his sister-in-law was still somewhere near the burning fire, and he had to act if she was to be saved.

"Luckily Wood knew where to find Mrs. Frear, and [we] arrived at the house just in time to get her into a baker's wagon, which Wood and I pulled for half a mile."

His sister-in-law was still distraught over the loss of her children, and grew even more agitated when they passed a wagon loaded with frightened children. Frear and Wood hurried away as quickly as possible, weaving around the piles of personal property abandoned in the road.

Once back at his sister-in-law's home, Frear tried to make her comfortable, aided by the capable hands and kind words of neighbors. The shock of his experiences began to set in, and he was overtaken by a pounding headache and fever. He had run the gauntlet of flames, risked his life several times in a futile effort to locate his young nieces and nephew, and barely managed to escape.

Imagine his feelings when, at four in the afternoon, the solemn, sad whispers in the house were replaced by loud, joyous shouts. A second later, Frear discovered that "word came from the Kimballs that the children were all safe out at Riverside." It was then that Frear could drag himself to a bedroom, climb into a bed, and pull a quilt over his head to shut out the fire.

As Frear slept, the fire went north with little opposition. House after house ignited and burned to the ground, leaving behind blackened foundations and charred heaps of wood. This area contained some of the city's largest, most stately homes, but the fire treated them with the same disdain it did the humblest wooden cottages on De Koven Street.

With the water supply gone, firemen could do very little unless they were near the river or lake and could draw water directly from those sources. Not even Hildreth's special talent with powder prevailed. After creating an effective firebreak in the south, Hildreth took his powder and scooted north to get in front of the fire. He took with him only two helpers, assuming that residents of the threatened blocks would eagerly volunteer. He tried to stop a number of men hurrying to escape, but none responded.

Sightseers peer at all that remains of the grand Tremont House. The familiar landscape of ornate buildings and elegant shops had been changed into one of charred black rubble and little else. (Author's collection)

"I grabbed hold of them, took right hold of them with more force than if I'd been sheriff . . . but they would leave me, just as soon as I would take my hands off them, and cut. The word 'powder' was a terror to them."

Finally, Hildreth, frustrated and weary, admitted defeat and headed home.

The same chaos and flight took hold of the northern section of the city. Alfred Sewell remembered the panic in the North Division: "Like an immense drove of panic-stricken sheep, the terrified mass ran, and rushed, and scrambled, and screamed through the streets. . . ."

Men who wrote about the Great Fire generally portrayed women as passive and helpless, waiting for their husbands, brothers, or some other man to save them. This seemed to go doubly for women who were wealthier. But if we look beyond the condescending references, a remarkable picture of strong and very active women emerges. Sewell might describe women as "weak and delicate [and] accustomed to no toil or trial" but they still managed to flee "with their arms full of treasures rescued from their doomed homes, and some even shouldered valises and trunks with the strength of strong men, and bore and dragged them through the crowd."

Or take the case of Julia Lemos. Lemos was a recent widow and the mother of five. In addition, she was taking care of her ailing mother and her elderly father, all while holding down a job as an artist at a lithographer's shop. At the end of September, Lemos found the burden of caring for all of these dependents overwhelming, and, reluctantly and tearfully, she placed four of her children in the nearby Half-Orphan Asylum. She hoped that her mother would recover quickly so that the separation would be a very short one.

Lemos found the situation extremely hard emotionally. While the chores were a bit easier, she missed her children and worried about them constantly. On the weekend of the fire, Lemos went to the asylum to get her children back, but was told that it was against official policy to release them just then.

The skeletal remains of a once-proud building on the Honore Block. A lone individual (just to the left of the lamppost) looks small indeed, standing so dangerously close to the ruins. (Author's collection)

Monday morning, Lemos woke to discover that the fire was heading toward their block. Her first course of action was to march to the asylum and demand that her children be turned over to her without any official mumbo jumbo. With her children in tow, she hurried home to organize their flight.

Since Lemos had little money, she went next door to her landlord's house and asked for the twelve dollars she had given him for that month's rent. He refused to give back any money, but when she didn't leave, he offered a compromise: he would take a load of her possessions to the prairie for the rent money. Lemos agreed and got two large trunks packed and on the wagon, plus a mattress and a featherbed.

At this point, her aged father balked at leaving the house, insisting that the fire would change direction before it got to them. Lemos paced the house, baby in her arms and four children following closely, all the time trying to convince her father to leave. She was looking out the door as others fled up the street when a woman hurried by with three children behind her. "Madam," the woman yelled sharply, "ain't you going to save those children?"

This question jolted Lemos into action. After insisting her parents leave the house, she guided the group out of the city and into the empty prairie where their possessions had been left. Thirty minutes after settling down for the night, wind-driven debris from the fire ignited the dry grass nearby, forcing them to abandon their things and retreat farther north. Lemos remembered feeling the heat of the flames on her back as she urged her parents and children along.

They stopped a mile from the first spot and formed a tight circle. Lemos cradled her baby in her arms, while her nine-year-old son, Willy, slept with his head in her lap. Suddenly, he began to cry.

"Willy, Mother is here," she whispered. "Do not cry."

"Yes, but, Mama," he replied, probably remembering a scary passage from the scriptures, "isn't this the Last Day?"

Lemos looked up. In the distance she could see the city on fire, the orange-red flames reaching toward the sky. She was about to

G.N. Barnard took this photo of the Van Buren Street Bridge. When bridges collapsed, their metal and wood beams clogged the river and made it impossible for ships to escape to Lake Michigan. (Chicago Historical Society)

say something comforting to Willy, when she saw a church steeple sag, then topple over and disappear into the dark smoke and flames. It certainly did seem like the Last Day, but she was sure of one thing: Despite all sorts of opposition, she had kept her family together and now they were truly safe.

Most of those escaping either headed for the Western Division or for the open prairie; almost thirty-thousand homeless people turned east and rushed toward the 230-acre Lincoln Park.

Lincoln Park was a long finger of wooded land stretching up the banks of Lake Michigan. To reach it, many people had to tramp through the site of the old German and Catholic cemeteries. Though most of the graves had been relocated, those of the very poor remained.

Soon the fire was nibbling at this peaceful strip, igniting the fence that ran along Clark Street, as well as trees and shrubs and the furniture brought there for safety. Not even the homes of the dead were safe as wooden grave markers burst into flames and some marble vaults cracked under the intense heat.

Frightened individuals huddled at the water's edge, while at least one group of desperate people constructed a crude raft and sailed it north. Surprisingly, there were few incidents of panic in the park despite the advancing flames. In fact, the crowd remained remarkably calm. One witness reported seeing a group of well-dressed people from a German saloon singing one tune after another while, a few tombstones away, a small congregation of Methodists held a prayer meeting.

The Great Fire would have burned until it ran out of city, then continued its hungry march across the prairie. Nothing the firemen or citizens of Chicago did seemed to stop the fire's insatiable quest for fuel. Then, around eleven o'clock, something happened that would later be called a miracle. Mixed in with the swirling smoke and falling embers, people felt a cool, damp substance on their cheeks. After several moments of shock and disbelief, they began shouting to each other with joy. What they were feeling was drizzle. As the hours crept by, the drizzle intensified, and by three

Almost thirty thousand people sought refuge in Lincoln Park, which was still home to a number of graves. There to greet them were somber headstones and recently abandoned household furniture. (Harper's Weekly, November 11, 1871)

in the morning, a steady rain was coming down. The drought that had lasted weeks and made Chicago as dry as kindling had finally broken.

Miles to the south and well away from the fire, Horace White peered from his cottage window. "There was no sleep for us until we heard the welcome sound of rain against our windows. How our hearts did rise in thankfulness to heaven for rain!"

Even those exposed to the rain in Lincoln Park must have rejoiced. The rain was chilly and uncomfortable, but it soaked the leaves and shrubs and grass and halted the fire.

One of the newly homeless was Mary Fales, who captured the general feeling of relief and salvation when she wrote, "I never felt so grateful in my life as to hear the rain pour down at three o'clock this morning. That stopped the fire."

The fire's rapid spread had been halted, but pockets of fire would burn in places all through the night and for days afterward. Contained at last, the fires could be dealt with, with real effect. But a new kind of drama was just beginning.

Nearly 100,000 people were now homeless. Many had been separated from loved ones during the fire and now had the daunting task of searching through a ruined city for them.

One of these people was Claire Innes. After escaping the alley, she "went along any street that was not burning, hoping to see someone familiar. Finally, I was too tired to take another step and gave up. I sat next to a pile of building stones and fell asleep. I woke only once and felt a light rain on my face and almost shouted I was so happy. There were no fires near, and no lights of any kind, so it was very dark. Someone was moving down the street, a man with a bundle who was using a stick to push aside wood and bricks. He put something — I could not see it — in the bundle, then continued searching the debris. The stones I was leaning on were still warm, but I began shivering and hoped the sun would appear again soon."

Joseph Battersby's photograph shows the complete devastation along the riverfront. The lack of details in the distance was caused by smoke from a fire at the coal works that burned for several days after the fire. (Chicago Historical Society)

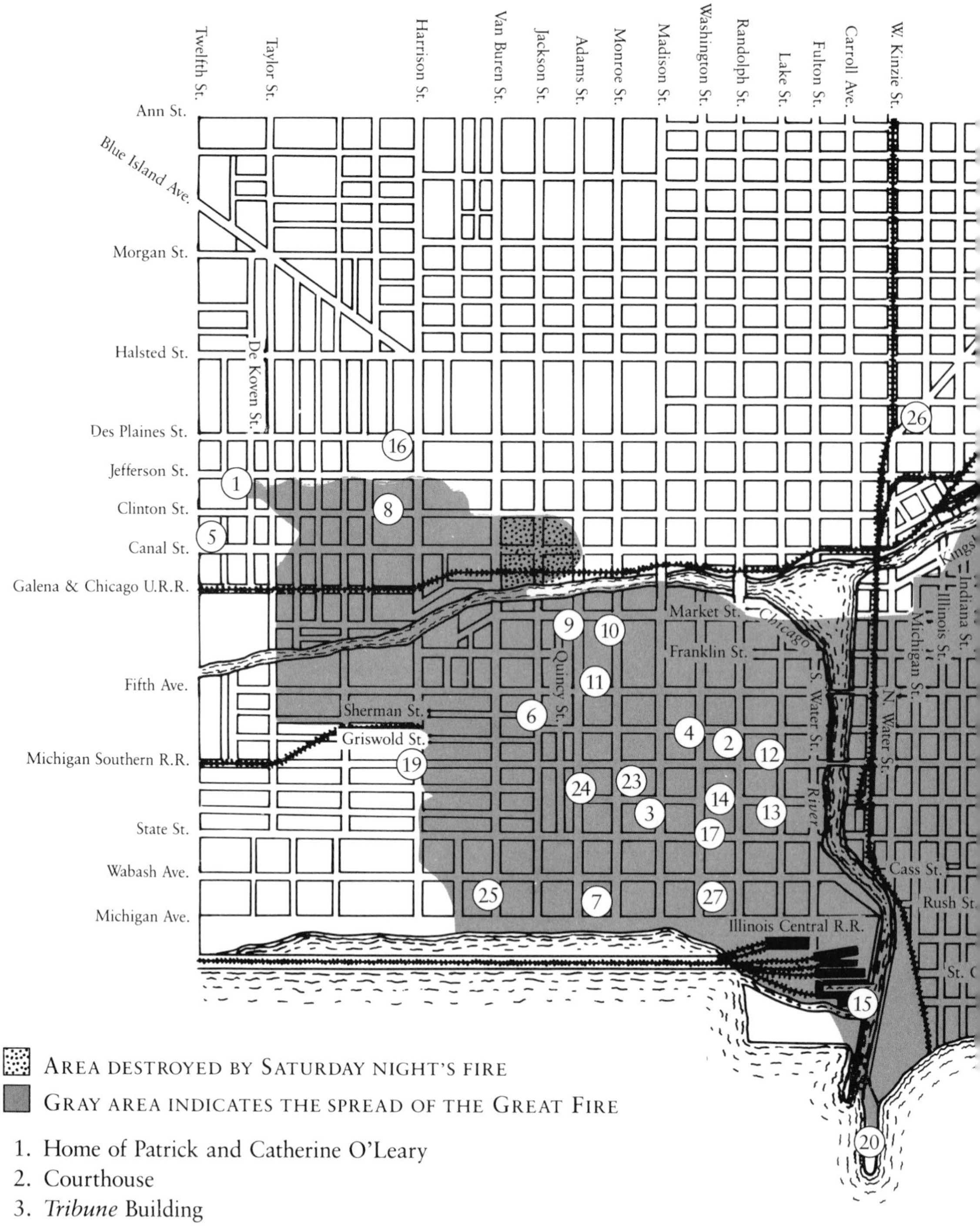
Twelfth St.
Taylor St.
Harrison St.
Van Buren St.
Jackson St.
Adams St.
Monroe St.
Madison St.
Washington St.
Randolph St.
Lake St.
Fulton St.
Carroll Ave.
W. Kinzie St.
Ann St.
Blue Island Ave.
Morgan St.
Halsted St.
De Koven St.
Des Plaines St.
Jefferson St.
Clinton St.
Canal St.
Galena & Chicago U.R.R.
Fifth Ave.
Sherman St.
Griswold St.
Michigan Southern R.R.
State St.
Wabash Ave.
Michigan Ave.
Quincy St.
Market St.
Franklin St.
Chicago
River
S. Water St.
N. Water St.
Kingsb
Indiana St.
Illinois St.
Michigan St.
Cass St.
Rush St.
St. C
Illinois Central R.R.
1
2
3
4
5
6
7
8
9
10
11
12
13
14
15
16
17
19
20
23
24
25
26
27

AREA DESTROYED BY SATURDAY NIGHT'S FIRE

GRAY AREA INDICATES THE SPREAD OF THE GREAT FIRE

1. Home of Patrick and Catherine O'Leary
2. Courthouse
3. *Tribune* Building
4. Chamber of Commerce Building
5. Bruno Goll's drugstore
6. Neighborhood where Claire Innes and her family lived
7. Horace White's house
8. St. Paul's Church
9. Armory
10. Gasworks
11. "Conley's Patch"

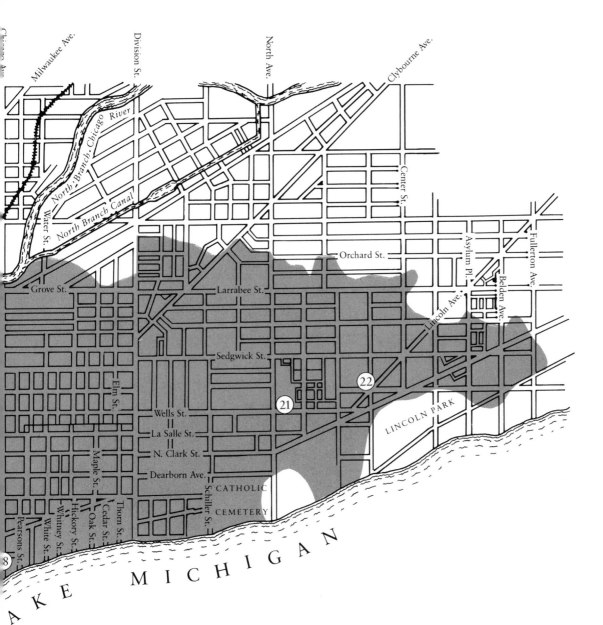

12. Sherman House
13. Tremont House
14. Crosby's Opera House
15. Grain elevator
16. Home of Alexander Frear's sister-in-law
17. St. James Hotel
18. Waterworks
19. Area dynamited by James Hildreth
20. Government Pier
21. Approximate location of Julia Lemos's home
22. Half-Orphan Asylum
23. Post Office and Custom House
24. New Honore Block

6 · "The Ghost of Chicago"

WHILE HUNDREDS OF FIRES were still burning on Tuesday, such as at the coal works, most of them were under control. Enough anyway for the rubble to have cooled somewhat, allowing citizens to explore what had been their city.

The burnt district was over four miles long and one mile wide; 17,500 buildings and 73 miles of street had been destroyed. Joseph Medill, the forty-eight-year-old publisher of the *Tribune*, surveyed the scene and recalled "more widespread, soul-sickening desolation than mortal eye ever beheld since the destruction of Jerusalem. The proud and stately city of yesterday . . . had sunk into cellars and basements. What had hours before been the mart of commerce was now an indescribable chaos of broken columns, fallen walls, streets covered with debris, melted metal, charred and blackened trees standing like spectres. Thousands of columns of smoke and enveloping tongues of flame still rose out of the tumbling ruins. . . . Great [grain] elevators had disappeared. The tall spires of churches, the Courthouse dome, the stately blocks that were the pride of the city and the admiration of visitors, the noted landmarks . . . everything had disappeared."

The fire was so intense that piles of pig iron melted like wax left in the sun, granite blocks split in two, and limestone and marble turned to powder and blew away. Arthur Kinzie had just moved back to Chicago on October 6 and was one of those who had fled with his family to the northernmost limits of the city. On Tuesday he and his wife and family decided to go to her sister's house on the South Side. "It was a strange sight as we passed through the burned district . . ." Kinzie recalled. "All the squares formerly built up solidly were now so many black excavations, while the streets had the appearance of raised turnpikes intersecting each other on a level prairie."

They had brought food and water with them and gave these out to the less fortunate along the way. During one stop "[we] encountered a very sick man. His wife . . . had obtained an old piano packing case, which she had placed on its side with the bottom toward the wind, and made a bed for her husband inside. A piece of candle fastened to a wire hung from the top, by the light of which she was reading to him. Her greatest trouble was want of water, and when we gave her a jugful her gratitude knew no bounds."

Another citizen had been out of town when he heard about the fire but managed to get back early on Tuesday. "Alighting from the [train] car, I took my way, in the gray dawn, through the damp and deserted streets. The rain was over, but the leaden clouds added a gloom to the already gloomy scene. . . . Its black, bleak desolation, its skeleton streets, its shapeless masses of brick and mortar, its gaunt and jagged spires, only remnants of walls but yesterday so proud and stately, stared at me from every point."

The man strolled along, and stopped at the river. "The turbid river was encumbered with masses of charred wood, with black hulks of vessels, and skeletons of fallen bridges. . . ." He looked all around him, dazed by the desolation. "[I] was alone with the ruins. ALONE WITH THE GHOST OF CHICAGO!"

But the citizens of Chicago soon realized that they didn't have much time to feel self-pity or even to reflect on the scope of the

A slightly elevated view looking along Clark Street (to the left). Most of the buildings have collapsed or been completely consumed; those still standing in the distance have been gutted and will have to be leveled. (Chicago Historical Society)

One popular form of post-fire entertainment was to compare before and after pictures of buildings. This picture shows what was left of the Chamber of Commerce Building. Other pictures of this structure appear on pages 18 and 59.
(Author's collection)

tragedy. While the fire no longer posed an immediate threat, their lives were still in jeopardy. The destruction of the Waterworks meant that the entire city's water supply had been cut off. In their book, *Chicago and the Great Conflagration*, Elias Colbert and Everett Chamberlin reported that as early as Tuesday morning a sense of desperation prevailed when "water-carts moving through the streets [were] being surrounded, every time they halted, by men in dressing-gowns and women in their meanest wear, bearing buckets and pitchers, to buy, at a shilling a pailful, the fluid which had suddenly become so precious."

This street was nicknamed the Insurance Block because so many insurance companies had offices on it. After the Great Fire, the insurance industry was in the same shape as these buildings. (Author's collection)

The city had no plan for a water shortage, and no real solution was found either. The few water wagons available made daily rounds, and people could obtain a limited amount of water at relief areas. But in the end, Colbert and Chamberlin admitted, "the people were obliged to supply themselves from the artesian wells at the western extremity of the city, or from the lake."

While the giant engines at the Waterworks were being taken apart piece by piece and examined for damage, temporary sources of power were sought. The two authors were impressed by one ingenious effort: "Locomotives . . . were rigged to pumps and set to work with all their might; and with such success that, in a week

When word of Chicago's disaster reached other cities, there was an immediate outpouring of relief contributions. In this bustling scene, food, clothing, and medical supplies are arriving at the Erie Railway Ferry-House in New York City. From here, a train will whisk them to Chicago where . . .
(Frank Leslie's Illustrated Newspaper, October 28, 1871)

after the fire, about a third of the people of the inhabited portions of the city had water. . . ." The water that flowed from the taps was judged to be "smokey but good."

Finally, the Waterworks' pumping engines were sent into motion and once again water pulsed through the giant arteries to all locations of the city. Sadly, no one had considered the hazards that might result from stagnant water in the pipes. It seems that "the pipes had become foul from the deposits of the muddy stream from the river. The consequence was much sickness for about two weeks, especially among children."

Of course, the biggest concern was how to deal with the nearly 100,000 homeless. Thousands were able to find temporary shelter in other parts of Chicago, while others simply abandoned the city altogether, preferring to start fresh in other cities. That still left nearly 65,000 people in desperate need of help.

General Philip Sheridan had been in town during the fire and immediately volunteered the muscle power of his troops to help distribute tents, and other emergency supplies. They must have worked very efficiently since one citizen, Jonas Hutchinson, wrote his mother that by midnight "the city [was] in darkness, no gas, [but] 50,000 army tents [were] being pitched to house the poor."

. . . volunteers will distribute items to the needy. (Frank Leslie's Illustrated Newspaper, November 4, 1871)

The emergency supplies of food and medicine would last only a few days at most, and most of the storage facilities for grain, meats, and beverages had been destroyed. There was a real possibility that tens of thousands faced starvation and disease.

Even as the fire burned on Monday, Mayor Mason officially established a relief society and appointed O.W. Clapp to distribute "charities from the unknown to the unknown." Clapp set about finding a large warehouse in an unburned section of the city and

Thirty thousand people called Lincoln Park home immediately after the fire. Tents and shanties dot the landscape as families attempt to settle into a new routine. To the left, near the tree, the water wagon dispenses its precious cargo. (Frank Leslie's Illustrated Newspaper, November 4, 1871)

had all contributions sent there. Meanwhile, Mayor Mason sent out urgent appeals for any sort of emergency relief. In this plea, Chicago was aided by the combination of telegraph and newspapers. As Colbert and Chamberlin observed, "there is a nervous system, of wires and printers' types, which connect all together, and . . . places Chicago in close *rapport* with all parts of the world. . . ."

News spread so quickly that by late Tuesday morning fifty train cars of provisions had already arrived. More — much more — would follow as cities throughout the United States organized collections of blankets, bedding, clothing, food, and cash. The impact of the disaster even reached Europe, where nearly one million dollars in cash was raised. One of those who read about the suffering in Chicago was a young Scot named Robert Louis Stevenson. He was a struggling writer at the time, but he was so moved by the newspaper reports of the suffering that he donated sixpence to the relief fund, all that he had in his pocket.

Claire Innes woke up on Tuesday, and went searching for something to eat. She didn't say where she went, but it seems she was successful because the next thing she said was, "After eating, all I wanted to do [was to] find our house — or what was left of it. Father or Mother might look there for me and I did not want to miss them as I did not know how to find them otherwise."

Claire wasn't alone in her confusion. Thousands of families had become separated in the mad scramble to escape the flames. Since there was no official way to help reunite families, everyone had to figure out their own course of action. One popular way of locating individuals was through the newspapers. The Wednesday morning editions of the papers carried scores of personal ads:

"Personal-information wanted of George Norman Beresford, who was in Chicago at the time of the fire. If this meets his eye, he is earnestly requested to communicate with his friends, who are in deep anxiety. . . ."

"Rev. J. T. Goodrich, stopping at the Metropolitan Hotel at the

With one hundred thousand people homeless, there was a scramble to find a place to live. Here, several families have erected shanties in the basement of a burned-out building. On the street above, General Philip Sheridan's troops patrol the area to keep rioting and looting under control. (Harper's Weekly, November 4, 1871)

time of the fire, is anxiously inquired after by his son, J.C. Goodrich, Tradesman's National Bank, Philadelphia."

"Mr. McLogan, 288 Laflin, has a boy 2 or 3 years old — speaks French."

"Will the gentleman who gave me the clock and picture on State st. Oct. 9 call at 258 Cottage Grove-av. Dr. Steere."

The most common way to find anyone was to inquire at every church or relief area, roam through Lincoln Park where thousands of people were staying, or wait at the location of a residence and hope the person showed up.

Claire Innes wandered through the burned district at mid-morning and was startled by the buzz of activity she found there. "The streets were crowded with wagons, coming and going, while people stood in groups looking at the smoking black heaps that were once houses and stores and churches. At one place, I saw a woman collecting pots and pans and arranging them on a stove, as if she were about to cook a meal. Next, I came upon several men gathered around a charred lump, and each man was shaking his head sadly. I did not want to think about what it might be, so I did not stop, as many passers-by were, but hurried along."

Of course, Claire knew exactly what "it" was. The fire, in addition to consuming buildings, sidewalks, and trees, had also taken a human toll. For many days afterward, bodies would be dug out of the rubble. A temporary morgue was set up in a tiny stable to handle the remains of the dead. The corpses — or what was left of them — were laid out in rows on the floor, and groups of four or five persons at a time were permitted to view them. Here, the true horror of the fire could be seen and felt.

Frank Luzerne went to the morgue on Wednesday night and,

A temporary morgue was set up in a stable on Milwaukee Street. A policeman tries to restrain the crowd while a man identifies the body of a relative. (Frank Leslie's Illustrated Newspaper, November 18, 1871)

after counting the number of bodies, he studied one by the flickering light of a candle. It was "the body of a young man partially clad in common workingmen's attire. The hair was completely burned off his head and body; the features were blackened and distorted with pain; the swollen lips were wide apart, disclosing the glistening teeth, and imparting a horrid grin, such only as agonizing death can stamp upon the face. The flesh was bloated to an astonishing size. The poor wretch was roasted alive."

In all only 120 bodies would be recovered, though officials estimated that nearly 300 people perished in the flames. Some of the unaccounted for probably fell into the river, and their bodies sank, never to be recovered. The rest had been cremated in the heat and their ashes sucked up by the swirling wind and blown away.

In the days following, the morgue became a busy place. Many people came to the morgue to search for missing relatives and friends. A far greater number came as sightseers, which is why policemen had to be stationed at the door to regulate the flow of visitors. In fact, the burned-out city became a magnet for the curious who clogged the streets to see the ruins and poke through the rubble for souvenirs.

Claire did not describe much after she passed the charred body. Instead, "[I] walked and walked and walked, one block after the other, all looking alike. I stopped to ask directions and was pointed in one direction, stopped again and was pointed in another. Finally, I came to our street — at least that was what I was told."

Even though she had walked through many blocks of burned-out buildings, seeing her block overwhelmed Claire. "Everything was gone. Where our house had been was nothing but a pile of brick and ash and nothing else. I looked all around, but nothing was the same. I had hoped my parents would be waiting for me, but no one was there. There was not much I could do except stay and wait all day."

Alone with the ghost of Chicago. (Chicago Historical Society)

Fire relics were a hot commodity after the fire; residents of Chicago and tourists alike wanted a piece of the historic event. (Frank Leslie's Illustrated Newspaper, November 11, 1871)

Most of Chicago felt the same way that Claire did — exhausted, stunned by the immensity of the damage, lost and alone. But others, many out of sheer necessity, had already found the energy to start over again. On Lake Street, for instance, Margaret O'Toole set up her small stand and began selling chestnuts. Hers was the first business to open in the burned-out area.

As the debris, bricks, and metal cooled, enterprising youngsters dug out melted candleholders, blackened plates and teapots, fused-together pieces of silverware, and sold them to tourists. Noticing this brisk trade in "fire relics," some adults joined the business. Thomas Bryan bought the 7,200-pound remains of the Courthouse bell (at $62\frac{1}{2}$ cents a pound), then sold it to H. S. Everhart. Everhart melted it down, and made the metal into souvenir bells and other trinkets.

Meanwhile hotel keepers prepared feverishly for the expected rush of lodgers (of both burned-out citizens and tourists). One man, George W. Gage, purchased the Gault House, the only large hotel left on the West Side, and began to furnish it. When he met Marshall Field on the street one day and told him that he needed a great deal of carpeting, the retailer sighed, informing Gage he wasn't sure he had "a cent in the world" to order it.

"Neither do I," Gage replied, "but there are thousands of people coming to see these ruins and I'm going to have a place to take care of them."

By Tuesday afternoon, the first loads of lumber were being delivered to the relief society. The building committee of the society gave enough wood to build a single-room structure to anyone who applied. And if the applicant didn't own any land, the city would rent ground on Michigan Avenue for temporary structures.

Two weeks after the fire, a building frenzy had already begun. Alfred Sewell strolled through the city, noting that amid the heaps of rubbish and ruin, "builders were busily engaged in constructing scores of one-story sheds for the temporary accommodation of merchants, and what was a fortnight ago one of the finest residence avenues in the world is now lined with board shanties."

One of the first business structures up and open was William Kerfoot's real estate office. The crudely painted sign on his shack could be seen as a guiding motto for the rest of the fire victims: "All gone but wife, children, and energy."

As the days crept by, more and more people shook off their despondency and began to rebuild their homes and businesses. The energy to start all over seemed to be catching. Take the case of Wilbur Storey, the owner of the *Chicago Times* newspaper. Immediately after the destruction of his business, he murmured, "The *Times* is dead. Chicago is gone, and I'm all through." Storey might well have given up entirely, except that all around him he saw fellow newspapermen scrambling to rent space and find type and paper. Soon, he, too, was filled with a new determination; Storey borrowed money from friends, dug out some old type from his barn, and had the *Times* publishing again on October 18.

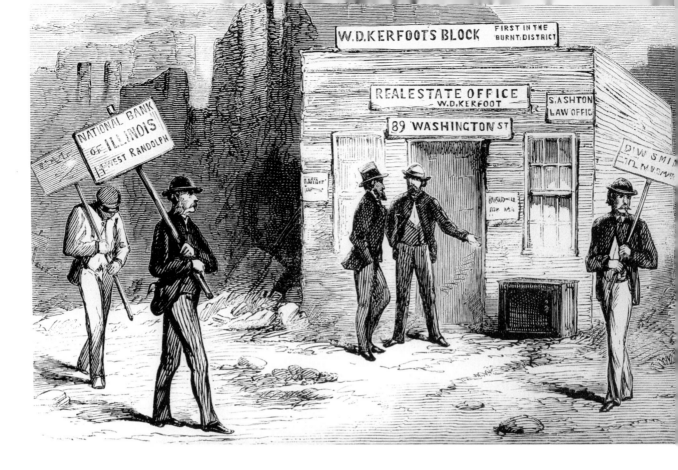

W.D. Kerfoot was proud to proclaim his real estate office the "First in the Burnt District." Since almost every business set up temporary offices outside the burned-out section of town, men with signs wandered the streets to advertise the new addresses. (Frank Leslie's Illustrated Newspaper, November 11, 1871)

In addition to the tiny shacks, substantial wood, brick, and stone structures were begun as well, and an army of workers emerged to do the job. Laborers combed the debris for undamaged brick (the only building material that survived the fire and could be reused) and hauled away everything else. All of the trash was carted to the lake and dumped; not only was Chicago swept clean of the fire, but a large landfill was created in the process.

The demand for carpenters and bricklayers soared, and farmers from as far away as 150 miles came to get jobs. Salaries also rose, with unskilled laborers commanding two dollars a day, while carpenters and bricklayers got anywhere from five dollars to ten dollars a day (amazing money back in 1871).

One month after the fire, Alfred Sewell took another hike

Carl Pretzel used humor to announce his departure for a new and more tranquil area: "Gone where the Woodbine Twineth." (Chicago Historical Society)

Two handmade signs grace the entrance to the ruined Insurance Exchange: one expresses a need for brick, while the other asks for the labor to put those bricks up.
(Chicago Historical Society)

through Chicago and returned in a jubilant mood. "A resurrection from the dead! Chicago is not hopelessly prostrate. . . . The number of temporary wooden buildings erected for the accommodation of business in the South Division had increased from the hundred or so we saw there two weeks after the fire, to several thousands, and the Lake front and some of the streets are literally lined with these structures, and in some localities trade is active. . . . Some large permanent brick edifices have already been reared on the scene of the ruins, and many others are in the process of erection. . . ."

A count done by the city building commission reported that by the end of 1871 there were over 6,000 wooden shanties, 2,000

The title of this photo might have been "Ruins and Reconstruction." The burned-out buildings in the rear seem to be watching as workers lay the beams for a new structure. Note the piles of brick that line the street. Brick was the only building material that survived the fire and could be reused. (Chicago Historical Society)

Amid the desolation there are some signs of life and resurrection. The shell of the building in the center was made of brick and survived the fire. Already new interior framing has been added. In time, the city would have so many buildings either being torn down or built that the period came to be called "Derrick Time." (Chicago Historical Society)

solid wood-frame buildings, and 500 structures of brick or stone already up or nearing completion. No wonder historian Alfred T. Andreas seemed overwhelmed when he reported: "It [was] common to see ten or a dozen or fifty houses rising at once; but when one looks upon, not a dozen or fifty, but upon *ten thousand* houses rising and ten times that number of busy workmen coming and going, and listens to the noise of countless saws and hammers and chisels and axes and planes, he is bewildered."

Not only was Chicago alive, not only was it going to rebuild, but many people predicted it would be bigger and better than before. One month after the fire, Alfred Sewell ended his discussion of Chicago with a stirring prediction: "The city will nevertheless rise again, nay, is already rising, like the Phoenix, from her ashes.

And she will, we believe, be a better city as well as a greater one, than she was before her disaster."

All of this was in Chicago's future. On Tuesday, Claire Innes was thinking only about her family and their whereabouts. "I do not know how long I waited, but it felt like a very long time. Smoke filled the air and made breathing difficult, and sometimes a great cloud of it would conceal everything. People were all around, but I did not recognize anyone and no one recognized me. A carriage went by with a woman and two gentlemen in it. The woman had on a beautiful coat and hat without a smudge upon them and I thought, for the first time, how shabby I must look."

It's possible that Claire, feeling self-conscious, decided to stroll down the block. Or she may have been bored. Whatever her reasons, she hadn't gone very far when she stopped short and stared at a familiar figure in the distance. "I saw a man pacing nervously — and it was Father! I had been waiting in front of the wrong house all along. You can imagine the reunion that followed and how happy I was to learn that Mother, Willy, Robert, Jr., and Charlotte had all escaped the fire and were now staying with a generous family who had opened their door to them."

Claire and her father hurried off to join the rest of their family. Claire did not write about this second reunion or of the deep emotions she felt. But as she passed through the blackened landscape and came closer and closer to them, she must have felt much the way another fire victim, Mrs. Charles Forsberg, did: "When we lay down, away from the crowd, and I knew I had my [family] safe, I felt so rich — I have never in my life felt so rich!"

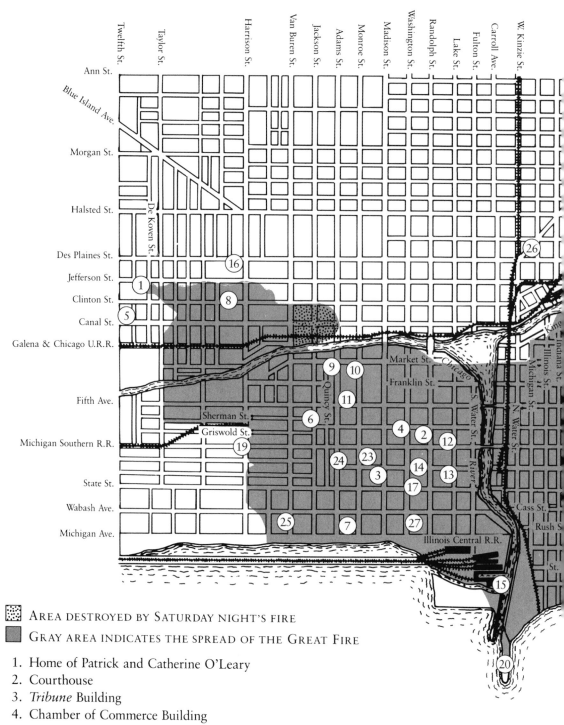

AREA DESTROYED BY SATURDAY NIGHT'S FIRE

GRAY AREA INDICATES THE SPREAD OF THE GREAT FIRE

1. Home of Patrick and Catherine O'Leary
2. Courthouse
3. *Tribune* Building
4. Chamber of Commerce Building
5. Bruno Goll's drugstore
6. Neighborhood where Claire Innes and her family lived
7. Horace White's house
8. St. Paul's Church
9. Armory
10. Gasworks
11. "Conley's Patch"

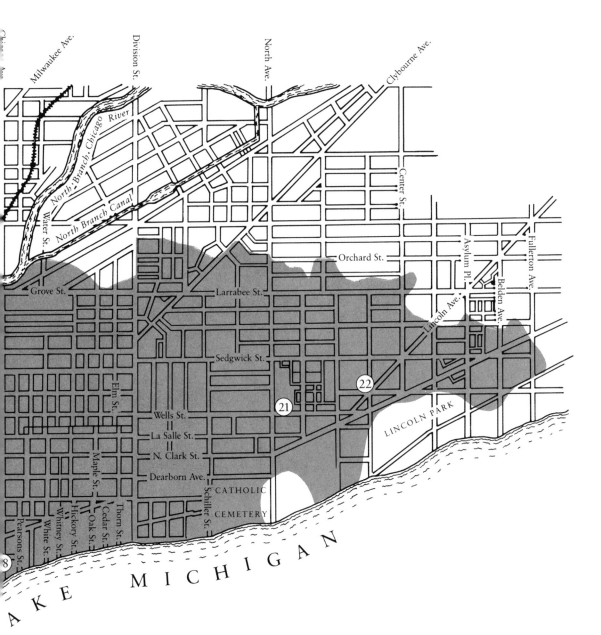

7 · Myth and Reality

BEFORE THE FIRE was completely extinguished, Chicago citizens were already demanding answers to some angry questions. Who was responsible for starting the fire? they wanted to know. How could professional firefighters have allowed the fire to run wild? And why did such panic and chaos result throughout the city?

The origin of the fire was never in doubt: It had begun in a barn at 137 De Koven Street. Other than this, there was absolutely no other detail that suggested how the fire started or who was to blame. But simply calling the Great Fire an accident did not satisfy some people, most notably the local newspapers. They demanded a culprit — and Catherine O'Leary was the handiest target in sight.

Chicago newspapers wasted little time before they pointed the finger of blame at her. On Monday, as the fire was burning furiously through the North Division, the Chicago *Evening Journal* managed to get out a limited edition. After describing the inferno, the paper stated: "The fire broke out on . . . De Koven Street . . .

being caused by a cow kicking over a lamp in a stable in which a woman was milking."

Considering the chaos of the city and the haste with which the paper had to be thrown together, the *Journal* might be forgiven for printing what was nothing more than gossip. Unfortunately, the paper never identified this statement as rumor and never bothered to retract it either. This "fact" was then picked up by other newspapers and amplified.

Artist W.O. Mull joined the popular movement to condemn Catherine O'Leary with this cartoon. In it a witchlike Catherine, along with a pail of milk and her lamp, have been knocked over by the kick of an angry cow. (Chicago Historical Society)

At that time, newspapers often launched vicious personal attacks, even going so far as to make up entire stories. For instance, on October 18, the Chicago *Times* ran a story that referred to Catherine O'Leary as "an old hag . . . whose very appearance indicated great poverty. She apparently was about seventy years of age and was bent almost double with the weight of many years of toil, and trouble, and privation." The story went on to state that Mrs. O'Leary had been angered at being removed from the county relief rolls and had sworn to get revenge. It then quoted her as admitting she had been in the barn on Sunday night at nine-thirty and that a cow kicked over the lamp.

What was accurate in this story? Nothing much. In 1871, Catherine was in her mid-thirties and had never received any sort of public relief. Why should she? Both she and her husband were hard workers and together brought in a respectable income. Besides, setting her own barn on fire made no sense, especially since the O'Learys carried no insurance on their property. As for the part about her having been in the barn at nine-thirty, the reporter seemed to have forgotten (or maybe he didn't really care) that by then the blaze had been going for almost forty-five minutes and that the barn had already been destroyed.

There were attempts to blame others. Those accused ranged from an anarchist group called the *Société Internationale* to a disgruntled fire extinguisher salesman who, it was alleged, was upset at sluggish sales and decided to demonstrate for Chicago why his product was vital. A few suggested that "Peg Leg" Sullivan had gone into the barn and had set it on fire while drinking. The editor of the Rushville, Indiana, *American* felt a higher being was responsible. After lamenting the destruction of the South by Sherman's army in 1864–65, he concluded his diatribe with "the destruction of property in the South was done purposely, by Northern soldiers, and compares exactly with the acts of the Goths and Vandals. . . . Chicago did her full share in the destruction of the South. God adjusts balances. Maybe with Chicago the books are now squared."

After Catherine O'Leary's name appeared in newspapers throughout the country, some people rushed to cash in on it. Here, an unidentified woman poses as Catherine on a viewing card sold by the Chicago Photograph Company. Catherine O'Leary never received a dime of the receipts. (Chicago Historical Society)

Such far-flung explanations never did stick. Late in November, a two-week inquiry was held by the police and fire commissioners concerning the fire. Many witnesses were called to testify under oath, including the O'Learys, their neighbors, and many of the firemen. It established clearly that the O'Learys were in bed when the fire began and that they were solid citizens. But to no avail. Idle gossip had hardened into established fact.

Cartoons continued to ridicule Catherine O'Leary and curious tourists came to gawk at the O'Learys' property. For added measure, the *Times* attacked Patrick O'Leary saying, "O'Leary

Sightseers visiting the O'Leary neighborhood. (Author's collection)

knew even less than she did. . . . [and was a] stupid-looking sort of a man, who acknowledged himself that he could neither read nor write." Feeling persecuted from all sides, the O'Learys eventually sold their property and fled the area.

The *Journal* summed up the sad fate of Catherine O'Leary in an article that appeared after the inquiry. "Even if it were an absurd rumor, 40 miles wide of the truth, it would be useless to attempt to alter 'the verdict of history.' Mrs. O'Leary . . . is in for it and no mistake. Fame has seized her and appropriated her, name, barn, cows and all."

As for why the fire spread, there were many reasons offered at the inquiry. Naturally, the exceptionally dry weather coupled with the strong wind was one. Another was the use of so much wood in the construction of homes, offices, sidewalks, and roads. Some mention was made of the understaffed fire department, aged equipment, the need for fireboats to patrol the river, and the fact that hydrants were placed far apart. Even the absence of an alarm being turned in at Goll's drugstore and the subsequent incorrect signals sent from the Courthouse were discussed.

Each of these was a real and important factor in the way the fire was able to race through the city unchecked, yet none was singled out as *the* cause. This didn't satisfy many people, and a second scapegoat soon emerged: the firefighters. And like the attacks on Catherine O'Leary, these often took on a nasty tone.

Typical of the criticism is what Alfred Sewell wrote in his book *The Great Calamity*. After criticizing Chief Marshal Williams as being "confused, bewildered, and utterly lost to usefulness," Sewell went on to state that "worse than all, his men . . . were, many of them, in a condition of 'demoralization' that was painful and sad to witness. . . . Adding to their fatigue, many of the firemen indulged freely on Sunday in the use of intoxicating liquors. . . . [To this] fact, as much to the wind or the drought, is to be attributed the so rapid spread of the flames as to place them beyond all control or power of mastery. A drunken Fire Department is . . . responsible for the destruction of Chicago."

This became the popular opinion despite the findings of the inquiry. After interviewing numerous firefighters and other eyewitnesses, the inquiry found that there had been drinking following the Saturday night fire, a ritual that was common not only in

One of the first things businesses did after the fire was to search through debris for their safes and any business ledgers that might have survived. Many of the safes were so hot when opened that oxygen entering them ignited and burned the contents. (*The Illustrated London News*, November 11, 1871)

Chicago, but in all cities back then. But there was no evidence that all or even many of the firefighters participated or that they drank heavily. In addition, there was no evidence that the effects of the celebrating either slowed the initial response or made the men less energetic once on the scene.

If some firemen did act strangely (moved lethargically, were clumsy, or had a glazed look in their eyes) on the night of the Great Fire, the best explanation is that they were completely exhausted from overwork and a lack of sleep. Half of Chicago's 185 active firefighters had spent all of Saturday night fighting a major fire, and many had come away with blistered skin, swollen eyes, and smoke-congested lungs. Instead of being able to rest and heal, these firefighters had to be on duty the next day even before the O'Leary fire broke out. Chief Marshal Williams, for instance, went to the Saturday night fire when the second alarm sounded and stayed until dawn the next day. He managed to get some breakfast and sleep, but was back at the scene of that fire to supervise the mopping up of embers in the early afternoon. Then he had to hurry to an early evening fire, which was quickly put out, before the signal for the O'Leary barn fire came in and he was off again.

The truth is that Williams and his firemen did everything they could possibly do to contain the fire and had followed established fire-fighting procedures as well. Witness after witness at the police-and-fire commission inquiry testified to this — but to little avail. The entire fire department joined Catherine O'Leary as an object of scorn.

Obviously, discovering the truth was not the most important thing when it came to condemning Catherine O'Leary and the firefighters. Something deeper, more pernicious was at work here: a wide division between the wealthy and the poor that was made worse by fear.

Before the fire, Chicago citizens viewed their city with justifiable pride. In 1833, when the village of Chicago voted to incorporate, it was a muddy little trading post with fewer than 100 inhabitants. During the intervening thirty-eight years, it had grown into a robust city of over 334,000 people and an industrial, commercial, and cultural center that rivaled the great East Coast cities, such as New York and Boston. Its reputation went far beyond the borders of the city; Chicago was known throughout the United States and the world as the Queen City of the West and the Gem of the

Prairie. It was, in every way, a shining symbol of the wealth and unlimited potential in the United States.

Then, in the space of a night and a day, this was all reduced to ashes. Gone. The fire had obliterated the heart of the city, its very center of business and culture, then had gone on to wipe out the residences of its wealthiest and most powerful citizens. In effect, the burned-out portions of the city were reduced to their 1830's primitive condition. Worse, the chaos and looting during the fire reminded people of the city's uncivilized pioneer days.

There was genuine concern that much of the city's industry would go elsewhere, especially to Milwaukee and St. Louis. A New Orleans newspaper painted a particularly bleak picture of Chicago's future when it announced that "a large portion of her population has deserted. . . . [and] no limited number of the more fortunate have seized upon the opportunity of transferring their business to St. Louis. . . . Its prestige has passed away . . . its glory will be of the past, not the present."

To counter such negative impressions, prominent business people launched an all-out public relations campaign. Great care was taken to point out that, while much of the business district had been leveled, many grain elevators still stood in other parts of town, rail and shipping service still existed, and numerous businesses had already set up temporary headquarters. More important, the spirit to rebuild was strong. The *Chicago Evening Post* would trumpet the city's vitality: "But when the raging fiend had died of plethora the old energy again came forth. . . . Citizens who had cowered and fled before it in awe arose bravely and said, 'We can conquer everything else.'"

Such emotional energy and civic spirit were admirable and would also prove to be absolutely true. Chicago would rebuild itself in a way that would astound the country and the world. But sadly, along with this spirit of community boosterism, another kind of public relations also emerged. To counter the idea that there had been mass panic and looting (that all of Chicago had reverted to its wild, lawless past and was therefore not a good

132

These workers are dwarfed by the mass of rubble that surrounds them. The job of cleaning up the mess was so massive that twenty years after the fire there were still some burned-out buildings scattered around the city. (Chicago Historical Society)

place in which to invest), articles and editorials appeared stating that there had been little or no rioting or looting. A noted landscape architect of Chicago, H.W.S. Cleveland, seemed indignant about such accusations: "There was little or no confusion, and nothing like panic. Everybody seemed cool and collected . . . and it is sufficient refutation of the absurd stories which have been circulating of outrages, lynchings, etc., to state the simple fact that my wife and her sister . . . were a long time walking about the streets in the vicinity of the fire . . . without ever a feeling of insecurity, or receiving an uncivil word from anyone."

The few problems that did arise, it was asserted, were caused by "certain types," namely the rising numbers of poor Irish, German, and Scandinavian immigrants.

When Horace White described the beginning of the fire, he said, "Vice and crime had got the first scorching. The district where the fire got its first firm foothold was the Alsatia* of Chicago. Fleeing before it was a crowd of blear-eyed, drunken, and diseased wretches, male and female, half naked, ghastly, with painted cheeks, cursing and uttering ribald jests as they drifted along."

Such a description of the O'Leary neighborhood was grossly unfair. It is true that there were no grand mansions there, and that it was very close to an industrial district. But by and large its inhabitants (mostly Irish, German, and Bohemian) were hardworking, honest people, who lived in modest frame houses of one and two stories.

This view, however, was not the one presented to the reading public in newspapers and books. What's more, there was the implication that the same sort of people described by White also caused the rioting in all parts of the city. Several hours after the fire began, Alexander Frear was in the South Side and reported, "The brutality and horror of the scene made it sickening. A fellow standing on a piano declared that the fire was the friend of the

---

*Alsatia refers to Alsace-Lorraine, a region in northeastern France that was annexed by Germany in 1871.

poor man." The next day, up in the more affluent North Division, Jonas Hutchinson was numbed by the spectacle he beheld: "As far as the fire reached, the city is thronged with desperadoes who are plundering and trying to set new fires. . . . Several were shot and others hung to lampposts last night. . . . The like of this sight since Sodom and Gomorrah has never met human vision."

Whether intentional or not, such references had the effect of distancing the "good and respectable" citizens of Chicago (that is, the better educated and wealthier) from the "bad" ones who had rioted. This latter group included not just vagrants and criminals, but anyone who happened to be poor or a recent arrival to the city.

To be fair, blaming the poor for the problems of a city (especially crime and disorder) was not at all unique to Chicago. Throughout the United States, those who controlled urban centers (business people, politicians, church leaders, and educators) tended to lump poverty, crime, and chaos together. In 1892, for instance, the Reverend Lyman Abbott of New York City pronounced that "at least one-tenth of the population . . . belong to the dependent, that is, to the pauper and criminal class. . . . In our great cities, poverty, ignorance, intemperance, and crime, the four great enemies of Republican institutions, thrive in frightfully overcrowded districts. . . ."

Such sweeping generalizations were routinely accepted, mainly because those attacked were not unified enough politically to counter the charges. In Chicago, city officials did nothing to soften the idea that the fire was caused by the city's poor. To do so would have forced people to look elsewhere for a culprit — a search that would have invited questions about the city's blatant lack of emergency planning. In fact, official policy after the fire actually encouraged the physical separation of the classes.

Stricter antifire building regulations were proposed for the burned-out areas, requiring the use of brick or stone. These materials were much more expensive than wood, and cost more to put up, and, thus, were beyond the means of poorer citizens.

The Marine Company Building rises up, clean and hopeful, at the corner of Lake and La Salle streets. Everywhere along the boulevard there are signs of rebuilding.
(Chicago Historical Society)

Few of the lower-middle class and poor families that lost their homes had fire insurance. Without cash, they were unable to hire carpenters and masons to rebuild their homes. The city made no arrangements to help less fortunate citizens procure loans necessary for the actual work.

A few efforts were made to protest the situation. Chicago's German community happened to be one of the few ethnic groups that was politically well-organized. On January 15, 1872, they staged a nighttime march to voice their anger over laws they felt were designed to penalize a single class, namely the poor. They feared (and justly so) that the new fire laws would eliminate any possibility of their owning their own homes and that, eventually, they would be forced into tenement buildings. But the feeling of the general public — bolstered by the press's focus on the "poverty-stricken" Catherine O'Leary and the "drunken" firefighters — wasn't sympathetic at all. As Professor Ross Miller notes in his book *American Apocalypse: The Great Fire and the Myth of Chicago:* "Subsequent 'antifire' legislation disproportionately penalized the working poor who owned their own wooden homes. Eventually they were allowed to rebuild in wood only outside the city's enlarged commercial district, but the stigma of their responsibility for the fire remained."

Another popular view that emerged was that the fire had been beneficial. An article entitled "The Effect of the Fire upon Real Estate" concluded that "Chicago property now stands better classified, and its future more distinctly marked, than could have been possible before the fire."

What about these new and improved buildings? Ironically, most structures put up immediately after the fire were little better than the ones that had burned down. The frenzy to rebuild was so great that architects had no time at all to draw lessons from the fire. It was not uncommon for work on a building to begin even *before* the architectural plans were completed. As a result, architects relied on old and dangerous habits, such as substituting wood for stone and decorating their buildings with wooden awnings, cupolas, and cornices.

Chicago probably would have been resurrected in the image of its old — and dangerously flammable — self, if two events had not intervened. The first was the failure of a major New York bank, Jay Cooke and Company, in September 1873, that set off a national depression. For six years after this, virtually all building ceased in Chicago. Then in July 1874, a fire (named the "Little Fire") destroyed millions of dollars worth of the post-fire structures. Only after this did the city outlaw the decorative use of wood on its buildings.

Six years would slide by during which little construction went on in the city. When the depression began to lift and another round of building began, a new kind of architecture emerged.

Spearheaded by visionary architects such as William Le Baron Jenney, Louis Sullivan, H.H. Richardson, Daniel Burnham, and John Root, the new architecture stripped away incidental ornamentation. Steel girders replaced wood-framing, exteriors were made of brick or granite, and designs favored straight, simple lines. What evolved was a style of building, known as "Chicago School," that was not just handsome, but truly fire-resistant.

Chicago had rebuilt itself in a way that dazzled its citizens and the world. But it had done so at a costly price: The poor were pushed farther and farther from the heart of the city — the center of wealth, hope, and potential. Even without the aid of a major fire, the same thing would happen to all other cities, though the process would be a gradual one, taking several decades. As journalist Thomas W. Knox noted in 1892: "There is a distinct tendency to the massing together of the rich in their own sections of the city. It is not merely that they find each other's society congenial, but that they consciously avoid and weed out the poor. . . . The poor are driven by inexorable necessity into 'the poor quarters' of the city, where they pull each other further down from all chance and hope."

Knox was talking specifically about New York City, but his concluding thoughts on this process could be applied to all large urban centers. "Fifth Avenue and the slums grow ever more hopelessly asunder. Fifth Avenue despises the slums, and the slums hate Fifth Avenue." These tensions and animosities would brew and simmer for many decades, and eventually they would result in urban unrest on a grand scale in the twentieth century.

In 1871, few people were able to look so many years ahead to see the deeper consequences of the fire and the city's rebuilding. What was clear to people like Catherine and Patrick O'Leary, Joseph Chamberlin, Claire Innes, Horace White, Alexander Frear, and more than one hundred thousand others, was that they had been touched by the Great Fire in a way that would change them and their city for all time.

Bibliography and Sources

SOURCES OF ACCOUNTS PRESENTED IN THIS BOOK:

Joseph E. Chamberlin's account of the fire first appeared in *Chicago and the Great Conflagration* by Elias Colbert and Everett Chamberlin, published by C. F. Vent, Cincinnati and New York, 1871.

Alfred L. Sewell's quotes come from a book he authored entitled *The Great Calamity*, published by Alfred L. Sewell, Chicago, 1871.

Horace White's recollections are from a letter he wrote to a friend and fellow newspaper editor, Murat Halstead, who printed it in his paper, the *Cincinnati Commercial* in October, 1871.

Alexander Frear wrote about his experiences for the *New York World* where they appeared on October 15, 1871.

Claire Innes described her adventure to a cousin in a letter, which appeared many years later in a book entitled *Recollections of a Bygone Era* by William E. Pendleton and Richard T. Hart, published by Cassell Petter & Galpin, New York, 1896.

OTHER BOOKS ABOUT THE CHICAGO FIRE:

Andreas, A.T. *A History of Chicago*. New York: 1884–86.

Angle, Paul M. *The Great Chicago Fire*. Chicago: University of Chicago Press, 1946.

Belcher, Wyatt W. *The Economic Rivalry Between St. Louis and Chicago 1850–1880*. New York: Columbia University Press, 1947.

Butt, Ernest. *Chicago Then and Now: A Pictorial History of the City's Development*. Chicago: Aurora, Finch & McCullouch, 1933.

Campbell, Helen, et. al. *Darkness and Daylight: Or, Lights and Shadows of New York Life*. Hartford, CT: A. D. Worthington & Co., Publishers, 1892.

Chamberlin, Everett. *Chicago and Its Suburbs*. Chicago: T. A. Hungerford & Company, 1874.

Cromie, Robert. *The Great Chicago Fire*. Garden City, New York: McGraw-Hill Book Company, 1958.

Hoyt, Homer. *One Hundred Years of Land Values in Chicago 1830–1933*. Chicago: University of Chicago Press, 1933.

Luzerne, Frank. *The Lost City: Chicago as It Was and as It Is and Its Glorious Future*. New York: Harper and Sons, 1872.

Kogan, Herman, and Lloyd Wendt. *Chicago: A Pictorial History*. New York: Dutton, 1958.

McIlvaine, Mabel. *Reminiscences of Chicago During the Great Fire*. Chicago: 1915.

Masters, Edgar Lee. *The Tale of Chicago*. New York: G. P. Putnam's Sons, 1933.

Miller, Ross. *American Apocalypse: The Great Fire and the Myth of Chicago*. Chicago and London: University of Chicago Press, 1990.

Pierce, Bessie Louise. *As Others See Chicago: Impressions of Visitors 1673–1933*. Chicago: University of Chicago Press, 1933.

Pierce, Bessie Louise. *A History of Chicago*. New York: Alfred A. Knopf, 1937–1940.

Sheahan, James Washington and George P. Upton. *The Great Conflagration*. Chicago: Union Publishing Company, 1871.

Zukowsky, John, ed. *Chicago Architecture 1872–1922: Birth of a Metropolis*. New York: Prestel-Verlag and the Art Institute of Chicago, 1987.

Index